MISSING
PERSIANS

❈

Gender, Culture, and Politics in the Middle East

Leila Ahmed, Miriam Cooke, Suad Joseph,
and Simona Sharoni, *Series Editors*

Missing Persians

Discovering Voices in
Iranian Cultural History

NASRIN RAHIMIEH

SYRACUSE UNIVERSITY PRESS

First Edition 2001

01   02   03   04   05   06   6   5   4   3   2   1

The paper used in this publication meets the minimum requirements of
American National Standard for Information Sciences—Permanence of
Paper for Printed Library Materials, ANSI Z39.48–1984.∞™

Library of Congress Cataloging-in-Publication Data

Rahimieh, Nasrin.

Missing Persians : discovering voices in Iranian cultural history / Nasrin Rahimieh.—

1st ed.

p. cm.—(Gender, culture, and politics in the Middle East)

Includes bibliographical references and index.

ISBN 0-8156-2753-X (alk. paper)—ISBN 0-8156-2837-4 (pbk. : alk. paper)

1. Iran—Civilization. 2. Iranians—Ethnic identity. 3. Discourse analysis—Social
aspects—Iran 4. Persian prose literature—History and criticism. 5. Iran—Intellectual life.

I. Title. II. Series.

DS266.R277 2000

955—dc21   2001020955

Manufactured in the United States of America

In memory of Taghi Modarressi,
whose place shall always be empty

Grieve not. Joseph who has gone astray
 will find his way to Canaan.
Grieve not. From the cell where sorrow dwells
 will spring a stand of flowers.

—Hafiz

Nasrin Rahimieh is associate dean of Humanities and professor of comparative literature at the University of Alberta. Her last book, *Oriental Responses to the West*, was published by E. J. Brill in 1990.

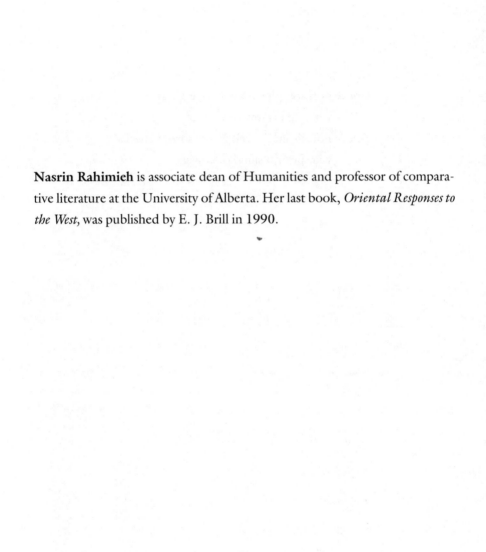

Contents

Preface

In the process of writing this book I have been fortunate to have the support of many friends, family members, and colleagues. I owe its very conception to the late Taghi Modarressi, whose novels, essays, and words of wisdom helped me come to terms with my own cultural displacement. In numerous telephone conversations and a few visits to the home he shared with Anne Tyler, Taghi urged me to look for answers to my personal losses in the writings of other Persians. Without his enthusiasm and encouragement I would never have embarked on this project. The year in which I wrote the first draft of *Missing Persians,* Taghi's perceptive insights and his infectious laughter became my lifeline.

After Taghi's untimely death in April 1997, I felt unable to return to all that reminded me of him, including this book. Although he had read and commented on an early draft, I could not fathom its completion without Taghi's voice inspiring me. It was the possibility of reconnecting to his voice, through translating his last novel he was able to complete before his death, that I could once again face the project he had sponsored. For this renewed hope, I am grateful to Anne Tyler and her confidence in me to provide her with the kind of translation Taghi would have wanted.

Closer to home, I am indebted to my husband, George Lang, whose own transcultural trajectory has made him my most patient audience. To George's flare for language I owe the title of this book, which he suggested during one of the long dinners we enjoy together with our four feline friends: Thèse, Esme-Shab, Nike, and Ti Xerxes.

Masood Jelokhani-Niaraki, a Persian who arrived in Edmonton in 1996 via a long detour through Japan, has been a most supportive and kind friend. Our animated conversations in Persian, his passion for Persian literature and culture, and his unique sensibilities have helped me face the missing Persian in myself. Listening to and reading the chapters of this book, Masood has provided me with invaluable insights I have incorporated into my text.

Among other Persian friends, always willing to listen to me and to share with me their extensive knowledge of our common heritage, I am particularly grateful to Mahmoud Gudarzi. The work of many other scholars of Persian literature, history, and culture has informed the writing of this book. Michael Beard, Ahmad Karimi-Hakkak, Julie Meisami, Farzaneh Milani, Hamid Naficy, Afsaneh Najmabadi, Kamran Talattof, and Ehsan Yarshater have been most generous providing me with the fruit of their own research and scholarship. Farzaneh Milani and Kamran Talattof took the time to read the manuscript and comment on it. I owe a special debt of gratitude to Farzaneh Milani for her generosity of spirit and wholehearted support at a difficult and crucial time.

My almost daily conversations with Daphne Read, my closest friend and most dear colleague at the University of Alberta, have been instrumental in my personal and academic life. Without her intellectual and moral support, I would not have had the courage to add my personal story to that of other missing Persians.

Among the numerous other individuals who have contributed to this book are graduate students with whom I have worked closely. My discussions with Christopher Gibbins, Manijeh Mannani, Nima Naghibi, Khatereh Sheibani, and Casey Williamson have often helped me articulate difficult concepts and ideas. They and many other students I have been fortunate to come into contact with have played a significant role in the shaping of my thoughts on this project. I thank Fred Ziegler of the University of Alberta Libraries for his prompt and kind response to my queries.

My mother, Oranous Hadidian, and my sister, Nahid Naini, have both influenced the completion of this project. Their constant asking about when I would finish writing infused me with a sense of urgency I in turn communicated to Mary Selden Evans of Syracuse University Press. Her repeated reassurances that *Missing Persians* had not gone missing and her enthusiasm and support for this project have been instrumental in the completion of my work.

I close these acknowledgements with a special word of gratitude to Liz Oscroft and Robyn Mott, who have seen me through indescribable torments of the soul and the body. Liz and Robyn have helped me rediscover the inner voice I believed to have forever lost.

A Note on the Text

I have used the Library of Congress transliteration system throughout this book without the diacritical marks. 'Ayn is represented by ' and hamzah by '.

All translations, unless otherwise noted, are my own. The epigraph by Hafiz is George Lang's translation.

MISSING
PERSIANS

Introduction

This book is about Persian travelers, renegades, converts, and transcultural migrants. The five figures to each of whom I devote a chapter all identify Persia as their country of origin and Persian, if not as their mother tongue, at least as the dominant language of the land configured variously as the sovereign political community or nation from which they hail.

The five characters at the center of the narratives I will examine also have in common a preoccupation with self-definition, prompted by departures from Persia, be it in actual or in metaphorical journeys. Recording their experiences of intercultural encounters in the form of memoirs, travelogue, autobiography, or social history, they give us glimpses of the process of passing from one linguistic and cultural territory into another. Not surprisingly, these passages and cultural makeovers sometimes trigger reexaminations of the notion of "home" and its forgotten or neglected religious, ethnic, and linguistic diversities. At other times, the encounter between the self and the other helps to reinforce Persian ethnocentrism and nationalism. What remains a constant, even in the least seemingly self-reflexive of these accounts, is the issue of identity, which at different moments of history finds varying designations and terms of reference.

What I put under the umbrella of Persian identity has not always been constructed and construed as a national identity in the modern sense of the term. As in other parts of the non-European world, in Persia nationalism arrived fairly late. The first stirrings of it can be found in the rhetoric of a popular movement in the first decade of the twentieth century that became known as the Constitutional Revolution (1905–11). It is in this moment in Persian history that we find the convergence of the three fundamental cultural conceptions Benedict Anderson identifies in *Imagined Communities*. Drawing on Walter Benjamin, Anderson attributes the possibility of imagining the nation along "horizontal-secular-transverse-time" (1991, 37) to the loss of a particular sacred language's ontological hold on truth, the erosion of the belief in the figure of the ruler as natural and inherent to the organization of a society, and the rise of a notion of time in which "cosmology and history were indistinguishable, the origins of the world and of men essentially identical" (Anderson 1991, 36). Persia was not imagined as a modern nation before the beginning of the twentieth century, but the very concept of Persia did exist in earlier times. As Ann Lambton points out in *Qajar Persia*, "such common feeling as there was among the people as a whole was religious, not national, and came primarily from the sense of sharing a common religious background. At the same time it was also in the sharing of their literary tradition that Persians, especially the educated classes, felt a common bond and a superiority to other peoples" (1987, 199–200). Furthermore, Juan Cole reveals that "the inventors of modern Iranian nationalism differed significantly with regard to whether they had a unitary or pluralist conception of the national self" (1996, 53). In Mohamad Tavakoli-Targhi's analysis the "refashioning of Iran and a rescripting of 'the people' and 'the nation' in Iranian political and historical discourses" was to take place through a "selective remembrance of things pre-Islamic" and a "dissociation of Iran from Islam" (1990, 77).[1]

I provide this cursory overview of the history of the concept of Persian identity to stress how it changes meaning and parameters over the course of time.[2] What matters for my analysis is a careful identification of the terms by

1. Mohamad Tavakoli-Targhi's "Contested Memories: Narrative Structures and Allegorical Meanings of Iran's Pre-Islamic History" sheds more light on the transformations that led to imagining Persia as a modern nation (1996, 149–75).

2. Sharokh Meskoob, in his *Iranian Nationality and the Persian Language*, presents a far more cohesive notion of Persian identity. Mehrzad Boroujerdi's *Iranian Intellectuals and the*

which at different moments of intercultural encounters Persians grasped the contours of their identity. But my study does not aim to chart the evolution of Persian nationalism. Throughout this work, my focus will be attempts at transculturation. My reasons for writing about Persians and their border crossings are related to my own personal and professional trajectory.

I was born into Persian, Turkish, or more accurately Azari,[3] and Gilaki, a dialect of Persian spoken in Gilan, a northern province on the shores of the Caspian Sea. Azari was not by any means an anomaly in the region where I grew up. There was considerable traffic between the predominantly Azari and the Gilani population until the Russian Revolution closed down borders. Much of my family history took place along those once fluid borders.[4]

As late as 1920, a memorial service for my maternal grandmother's first husband was held in Lankeran, his hometown, today part of the Republic of Azerbaijan. The family was so used to crossing from one side to the other for weddings, funerals, and visits that the newly instituted visa requirement, coinciding with Russian revolutionary turmoil that spread to Persia and later re-

---

West: The Tormented Triumph of Nativism, in contrast, argues that "modern Iranian intellectuals' concept of the 'self' has been historically constrained by their perceptions of a dominating Western other" (1996, 176).

3. In his *Azerbaijan: Ethnicity and Autonomy in Twentieth-Century Iran,* Touraj Atabaki points out that Azari initially designated the language spoken in the region of Azerbaijan before the "great migration of Turks into Asia minor in the eleventh century" (1993, 9) and that "The spread of Azerbaijani, the local form of this branch of Turkish, was so successful that by the beginning of the sixteenth century when Shah Isma'il established the dominion of the Safavid dynasty in this region, there was scarcely any trace of the old Azeri, and by then Azerbaijani was 'the common language of the people of Azerbaijan' " (10).

4. The redrawing of these borders has a long history. In *An Historical Geography of Iran,* W. Barthold writes: "A part of Gilan with the town of Rasht was conquered by Peter the Great in 1723; according to an agreement concluded in that same year, Iran also ceded to Russia Mazandaran and Astarabad, but neither region was really occupied. . . . In 1729, Russia officially renounced Mazandaran and Astarabad, in 1732 it returned Gilan and . . . even Baku and Darband, which were, however, reconquered at the beginning of the nineteenth century" (1984, 236).

sulted in the formation of a short-lived socialist republic in Gilan,[5] took them by complete surprise. They finessed their way back to Gilan, but that was the last time my grandmother set foot on Azerbaijani soil.

From this grandmother I never knew, I have inherited pre-revolution Russian banknotes she clung to all her life in the hope that one day they would regain their value. For years she ended her prayers with "Dear God, please make my money real again." Her dreams never became reality, but she succeeded in passing on to generations of her offspring a persistent longing for border crossings.

In my imagination, I attribute this grandmother's border fetish to her father's career first as harbor master and later as *kalantar,* or sheriff, of the port of Anzali, our hometown on the Caspian shore. The man she married, after the death of her first husband, my own grandfather, she met thanks to this father's status. As a renegade of sorts, my grandfather had to leave his hometown of Baku, cross over to Persian soil, and seek refuge in my great-grandfather's house where, family legend has it, he fell in love with his savior's daughter.

My mother's family gave me a sense of what it meant to be attached to more than one land, language, and culture and instilled in me an intuitive understanding of the borders of national identity as ever changing and negotiable. My maternal relatives continued to speak of "across the water" long after they were cut off from family members in what became the Soviet Azerbaijan. Radio Baku gave them the link letters, delivered after a hiatus of some forty years, later recreated. I have a vivid memory of the first packet of letters delivered to my aunt's house. The letters were written in Azari, evoking a time when my grandmother was still alive. Much had changed and had to be announced to the Azari relatives, eager to visit and reestablish old ties. But it would take years before any of them would cut through red tape, board a ship, and reanimate the past.

By this time, I was already far away from home, having embarked on a few

---

5. Family lore is rather careless with dates. I refer the interested readers to Cosroe Chaqueri's meticulous and enlightening *The Soviet Socialist Republic of Iran, 1920–1921.*

border crossings of my own. But even before leaving Persia, I had been instructed in my parents' dual tradition of compulsive shuttling between languages and cultural affiliations, on the one hand, and embracing Persian national identity, on the other.

The first school I was sent to was run by Armenians; the principal and most of the teachers spoke an accented Persian I adopted as my standard. Here I acquired more than a desire to speak Persian as my teachers and friends did; my imagination was fueled by the differences, real and imagined, between myself and Armenian classmates with their own separate language, rites, and rituals. My most cherished memory from those early days is of a small chapel, in the school yard, where periodically funerals and other ceremonies had to be conducted during school hours. Because I, a Muslim student, would not normally have access to the chapel, I longed to see its interior and enter this other world just beyond my reach. During one recess, my desire was fulfilled. While running after a ball that had strayed as far as the half-open chapel door, I was granted my first and last glimpse of the plush and perfumed chapel. Of that dim interior I have retained the deep reds of the carpets, the darkly stained pews, and the rhythmic swinging of the incense burners. Long after the chapel door was shut, I continued to fantasize about belonging on the other side. Joining in the Armenian celebrations at school, mouthing the lyrics of songs I did not understand, and learning to play a few tunes on the piano constituted my first ventures into embracing otherness.

At other schools I subsequently attended, the Armenian accent was replaced with a Gilaki-inflected Persian. This new way of speaking Persian was the next best thing to being surrounded by Armenian. It made it possible for me to carve out a different form of hyphenated, albeit more communal, identity.

I received my first introduction to English in this same local accent. The sweltering afternoon on which our English teacher read to us from our primer about Mark Twain's life set me off in a new imaginative direction. Hearing in my teacher's Gilaki-accented English about Mark Twain inspired me to imagine this American lurking in the lagoons of my hometown of Anzali. True to my family history, I would associate any body of water with imaginary expeditions. What has always facilitated these expeditions of the mind for me has been my entry into a new language.

On the linguistic map of my childhood, my parents drew other boundaries. They imposed Persian as a neutral medium of exchange in a household where the maternal Azari competed with the paternal Gilaki. Exempting themselves from this linguistic stricture, my parents spoke to each other in Gilaki, but we, their two daughters, had to learn to answer in Persian. Not only did my sister and I not rebel against this linguistic pact, we became its enforcers and demanded that our mother and her relatives speak to each other in Persian so that we could understand them, or more accurately so that we could forget the Azari we understood instinctively. In the process of becoming Persian, we had to accept Azari and Gilaki as languages of minority.

Our family effort notwithstanding, Gilaki could not be relegated to the margins. It was the language spoken outside classrooms and government offices, but Azari was by and large banished from all but the most intimate gathering of my mother's family. Paradoxically, the more my sister and I embraced Persian as our adopted mother tongue, the more we became metaphorically exiled from part of our immediate family. The very programmed attempt to graft us onto a unilingual Persian identity inadvertently caused us to replicate within the boundaries of home our maternal relatives' sense of exile. This heritage has underwritten much of my life history. Even now, my relationship to language is determined by a peculiar need to simulate conditions of alterity,[6] or a sense of being divided within.

An ever-present internalized notion of duality has prompted me to embark on relearning Azari in the Canadian setting I now call home. Armed with teach-yourself-Turkish tapes and grammar books, I rejoice at the slightest recollection of a long forgotten word or turn of phrase. That now English has replaced the register of dominance Persian once occupied is evident in the

6. The term "alterity" has a long history traced by Michael Taussig in his *Mimesis and Alterity*. My use of the term evokes a sense of awareness of linguistic, cultural, and psychological differences from others that constitute the notion of the self.

process through which I arrived at a knowledge of English only to destabilize my relation to it through other languages.

I learned to speak English while living as an exchange student with an American family in Connecticut. No sooner had I acquired a basic grasp of English than I found myself in Switzerland, where other languages had to be taken into account. By the time I arrived in Canada, taking up French and German in the English-speaking part of the country seemed not so far-fetched. I was not just making up for the discarded Azari and Gilaki, I was un-consciously recreating the linguistic diversity and complexity of my origins. Learning other languages was an expression of my sense of dislocation as well as an acting out of the intuitive perception, inherited from my displaced rela-tives, that linguistic and cultural identity was open to negotiation.

At long last, I made a virtue out of my linguistic and cultural restlessness by studying comparative literature, a discipline that, in Emily Apter's words, "is unthinkable without historical circumstances of exile" (1995, 86). Even though the traditions of comparative literature were steeped in European lan-guages and literatures, I found myself at home in comparative literature's "ex-ilic aura" (Apter 1995, 94). Allowing me to move beyond the confines of one national language or literature, comparative literature seemed best suited to my personal need for transcultural movement and migration.

For years I read any immigrant writer I came across. In 1989 my partici-pation in a gathering of Persian writers in exile brought me into renewed con-tact with issues of Persian identity. The work of Persian immigrant and exile writers opened up new arenas of inquiry and learning. A few creative re-sponses, foremost among them Taghi Modarressi's, reoriented my thoughts toward the kinds of paradoxes I had lived in my own upbringing and later come to associate with the experience of immigration and exile. In Modar-ressi's essay "Writing with an Accent," I found a clear articulation of the con-dition of being a stranger to oneself:

> [M]ost immigrants, regardless of the familial, social, or political circum-stances causing their exile, have been cultural refugees all their lives. They

leave because they feel like outsiders. Perhaps it is their personal language
that can build a bridge between what is familiar and what is strange. They
may then find it possible to generate new and revealing paradoxes. Here we
have our juxtapositions and our transformation—the graceful and the awkward, the beautiful and the ugly, sitting side by side in a perpetual metamorphosis of one into the other. It is like the Hunchback of Notre Dame trying
to be Prince Charming for strangers. (1992, 9)

This vision of a "perpetual metamorphosis" made it possible for me to think
alterity in terms other than borders and boundaries. "Juxtaposition" and
"transformation" obviated the need for a simple binarism of self and other,
Persian and Azari, Persian and Gilaki, English and French, or English and
German. However, this intellectual resolution was soon put to the test.

Border problems of another kind reentered my professional life as comparative literature, like many other disciplines, was asked to rethink itself. The
anxiety over the loss of disciplinary and territorial status in my small corner of
academia was part of a larger problem amply discussed in a report commis-
sioned by the American Comparative Literature Association published, along
with several responses to it, under the title of *Comparative Literature in the
Age of Multiculturalism*. My own experiences of the academic territorial bat-
tles coincide with Emily Apter's representation of them, in an essay included
in the volume I mention above, as "a poorly masked strategy for marginalizing
the latest arrival in town (there are obvious analogies to the anti-immigration
stance of second- or third-generation immigrants, concerned to keep out recent arrivals)" (1995, 87). The worry about what was the proper domain of
comparatism and who belonged to the discipline had all the unhappy reso-
nances of the binarism I thought to have left behind in favor of "perpetual
metamorphosis."

The effect the debates over the future of the discipline of comparative literature had on me was to make me question my own place in it. The view I
came to adopt was not unlike what Mary Louise Pratt describes in her contribution to the report, "Comparative Literature and Global Citizenship," in
which she bemoans the absence of "excitement, curiosity, and passion" in the

comparatists' encounter with the new challenges facing their discipline (1995, 61–62). The rhetoric of loss and devastation so many of my co-disciplinarians adopted around this time reinforced my sense of alienation and ultimately led to a personal crisis of sorts. My instinct to adapt, to see myself through change, and to survive seemed drastically diminished. After months of watching myself come unraveled, both physically and psychologically, I began to make connections to a half-forgotten and buried medical trauma I had suffered at the age of ten. The links between my sense of being a stranger to my body, a stranger to language, identity, and even my profession prompted a better understanding of my responses to different types and levels of exile. This in turn initiated a process of personal and professional recovery. I returned to my intuitive grasp of the position of the outsider as both enabling and destabilizing. Instead of being locked in my traumatized state, I undertook a new journey toward metamorphosis.

My first step out of this crisis was to abandon the disciplinary and institutional debates, to withdraw from them to rediscover the excitement, curiosity, and passion I had been sorely missing. What emerged from months of reading was a decision to redraw the boundaries of my imagination and to return to paradoxes of identity in the history of Persian encounters with the West. The point was not lost on me that my new interests were a form of return to origins, but reterritorialization[7] is not an unexpected repercussion of territorial disputes. This return to the self was also a means of coming to terms with an internal voice, which the many registers of my exile had suppressed. Admitting to my being a missing Persian was the first stage in a process of rehabilitation, punctuated by a rediscovered need to hear and read Persian. My native tongue, even my accented variety of it, no longer evoked distance and silence.

I began by reading travelogues written by Persians at different moments in history, initially asking myself how Persian travelers had come to terms with other cultures and how their experiences of alterity had shaped their percep-

---

7. I borrow this term from Gilles Deleuze and Félix Guattari's *Kafka: Toward a Minor Literature*. For them, reterritorialization is associated with reconfigurations of social, political, and psychological forces that can destabilize or deterritorialize established and hegemonic patterns.

tions of themselves and the world beyond their borders. What I labeled for myself "encounter narratives" soon spilled over from travelogues into other genres. Under the guise of memoirs and diaries were presented reflections on questions of identity and self-definition. I came across instances of intense curiosity about the other, desire to discard one identity for another, attempts to renegotiate Persian cultural identity, and self-conscious enactments of newly adopted models. Underlying these disparate narratives was an unstated, or in some cases understated, understanding that encounters with outside cultures demanded a certain degree of performance. The need to embody a cultural or national identity, if only for the benefit of an exotic audience, sometimes became the catalyst for self-examination and change. Stepping beyond Persian borders did not necessarily produce the type of reflections Montesquieu attributed to his fictional characters in *Persian Letters,* but it did inspire many a Persian traveler to ponder questions not unlike that asked of one of Montesquieu's fictional Persians: "How can one be Persian?" (1973, 83). It was the gamut of responses to the crucial questions of identity that intensified my interest in Persian narratives of encounter with the West. In them, I saw facets of my own journeys and the personal dilemmas they had instigated. Even more importantly, my imaginative encounters with these missing Persians reaffirmed the type of "tolerance for ambiguity" Gloria Anzaldúa attributes to the new *mestiza* in her *Borderlands/La Frontera*: "She learns to juggle cultures. She has a plural personality, she operates in a pluralistic mode—nothing is thrust out, the good, the bad and the ugly, nothing rejected, nothing abandoned. Not only does she sustain contradictions, she turns ambivalence into something else" (1987, 79). A desire for preserving plurality both in genres and in historical periods is reflected in my choice of missing Persians.

I begin this study with a seventeenth-century diary of a Persian's travels through Europe, *Don Juan of Persia: A Shi'ah Catholic.* The original Persian, lost in the annals of history, was written by Uruch Beg,[8] a member of an embassy sent by the Persian king to European powers to seek alliances against the

---

8. In "European Contacts with Persia, 1350–1736," Laurence Lockhart notes that the name Uruch is possibly a corruption of Uluch (1997, 387).

Ottoman Turks. When the author converted to Catholicism in Spain, the original text underwent its own conversion, resulting in a cultural and textual hybrid overladen with intriguing questions about the contesting voices, which claim to speak for a missing Persian.

My next chapter is devoted to *Safar Namih-i Shikagu* (Chicago Travelogue), a work whose authorship is not at issue. A record of Haji Mirza Muhammad 'Ali Mu'in al-Saltanah's tour of Europe and the United States, where he visited the 1893 World Columbian Exposition, this work highlights the ways in which its author's perceptions were mediated through the interpreters who accompanied him at various stages of his journey. What is particularly interesting in Mu'in al-Saltanah's seemingly "objective" accounts, written from a fairly anchored sense of self-identity, are the moments in which he struggles against the experience of liminality.

For 'Abdullah Mustawfi, the figure at the center of the next chapter, the encounter with the other began when he received a diplomatic post in St Petersburg in 1904. Mustawfi's *Sharh-i Zindigani-yi Man* (Description of My Life), the three volumes of which were written between 1942 and 1947, reveals a fascination with what he conceptualized as "European culture." Mustawfi's transcultural experiences and the story of his life are integrated into a social and administrative history of the Qajar era. The blending of life writing and social history in many ways veils the narrating self,[9] but attempts at transforming the Persian self vis-à-vis the European fuse the life of the individual with that of an entire generation faced with new questions about Persian identity.

The passion with which in the early twentieth century Persians addressed the prospect of reenvisioning themselves is reflected in *The Memoirs of Taj*

---

9. Tracing the origins of the term "life writing" to the eighteenth century, before the terms "biography" and "autobiography" gained currency, Marlene Kadar argues that "life writing has always been a more inclusive term, and as such may be considered to have certain advantages over 'biography' and 'autobiography.' Thus life writing, put simply, is a less exclusive genre of personal kinds of writing that includes *both* biography and autobiography, but also less 'objective,' or more 'personal' genres such as letters and diaries" (1992, 4).

al-Saltanah, written in 1914 by the daughter of one of the Qajar kings, Nasir al-Din Shah, who himself traveled to Europe on more than one occasion and kept diaries of his journeys. Interestingly, while the daughter never had the opportunity to see Europe, her passion was no less ignited by what she learned about European cultures through her readings. She became an armchair traveler and traversed the borders of her homeland in her imagination. What she read in literature and history began to form such impressions on her that she melded herself into an imaginative world riddled with the paradoxes of Persian modernity and its complex configurations of gender identity.

The uneasy performance of identity at the crossroads of nation and gender form the basis of my last chapter, focused on *Persia Is My Heart,* an intriguing text copublished by Najmeh Najafi and Helen Hinckley. The collaboration between the Persian and the American lasted over a fourteen-year period in which they coauthored two other books: *Reveille for a Persian Village* and *A Wall and Three Willows.* In a manner of speaking, all three books trace Najmeh Najafi's life through her upbringing and youth in Persia, a period of study in the United States, and her return to her homeland as a social worker involved in work done under the auspices of American foreign aid organizations. My interest in reading *Persia Is My Heart* was provoked by the way in which Najmeh Najafi's identity is self-consciously staged for the benefit of her American readers.

In reading these five different negotiations of identity across linguistic and cultural divides, my aim is not to arrive at a representative or comprehensive history of Persian encounters with the West. There are numerous Persian diaries, political and personal memoirs, and travelogues that I shall be leaving out of this study. Historians, political scientists, and sociologists have already analyzed much of this material and have provided extensive studies from which I have benefited immensely in my endeavor. I hope to reflect my indebtedness to the depth and breadth of this scholarship throughout this book. The aim of my own more modest project is to investigate the multiple forms of self-expression that emerge in liminal spaces. I use the term self-expression instead of memoir, life writing, or autobiography to signal both the multiplicity of the genres included in my study as well as the critical debates about the existence of some of these genres, particularly autobiography, in Persian letters. Although I do not wish to argue against the work of the historians and critics of Persian literature, I do propose to situate some of these culturally specific discussions within the current criticism on the types and limits of the genres clustered, albeit loosely, under the rubric of life writing. My objective is not to establish new criteria or generic codes for instances of Persian writing. Instead, I hope to show how a reexamination of the very critical tools we use can help us find unexpected and anomalous modes of writing in sources that resist easy definitions. History of a literature is also a history of its criticism.

In the fourth volume of *A Literary History of Persia*, the first systematic attempt at Persian literary historiography, Edward Granville Browne devotes a section to "Biography, Autobiography and Travel" in which he attests to the Persian penchant for biographical writings of a certain kind: "More often such works treat of the biographies of some particular class of men, such as Ministers, Physicians, Poets, or Theologians; or they follow a geographical or a chronological arrangement, merging on the one hand into geography and on the other into history" (1959, 447). Jan Rypka's *History of Iranian Literature* points out: "biographies of individual persons and autobiographies are rare" (1968, 449). In "Half-Voices" William Hanaway provides an insightful description of the intertwining of the form and function of other modes of writing about life: "Biographies of another sort are found in *tazkarehs*, the biographical compendia of poets, sufis, and other classes of persons. The lives of 'saints' and panegyric odes generally present the same sort of model, emphasizing the moral and didactic value of the life for the reader" (1990, 60). The transmission of ethical concerns to biography would seem to emphasize the extent to which this genre is anchored in literary and rhetorical conventions based on a feudal or princely social order in which the individual's place in the community takes precedence over the individual.[10]

In *Veils and Words: The Emerging Voices of Iranian Women Writers,*

---

10. For discussion of these literary conventions, see Julie Meisami's *Medieval Persian Court Poetry*.

Farzaneh Milani extends this analysis to the more recent chapters of Persian literature: "Modern Persian literature, which has incorporated many Western literary forms, has avoided to a large extent one of the West's most popular genres. Avoiding voluntary self-revelation and self-referentiality, most Iranian writers have turned their backs on autobiography" (1992, 202). Milani finds this reluctance toward autobiography rooted in cultural norms: "In Iran, where not only has art been mainly impersonal but also where an individual's identity is closely tied to the community and where use of the first-person-singular pronoun is still hard for people and is often diffused a bit by *we*, writing an *I*-book is not an easy task. A most popular explanation offered for not writing autobiographies is a certain sense of humility, a shyness about one's own importance and accomplishments" (1992, 206).[11] At times, however, we find this humility incongruously juxtaposed with a public persona, the presentation of whose achievements verges on vanity. This predilection for an exaggerated sense of one's good deeds might well be rooted in the tradition Hanaway traces in Persian biographical writing. Such paradoxes highlight the complexities of the self I shall turn to in my analysis.

What Milani and Hanaway, among other critics, conclude about the absence of autobiographies in Persian underlines a different concept of subjectivity that does not lend itself well to the demands of a genre that "owes a great deal to post-Renaissance thought about the worth of an individual and the uniqueness of a human life" (Hanaway 1990, 61). This view is echoed by Georges Gusdorf: "it would seem that autobiography is not to be found outside of our cultural area; one would say that it expresses a concern peculiar to Western man" (1980, 29). It is worth bearing in mind the conditions that in

11. In his introduction to *Middle Eastern Lives,* Martin Kramer identifies a similar avoidance of confessional narratives on the part of Middle Eastern subjects. He points to "a certain sense of propriety and privacy common to most of the Middle East" that "transforms self-revelation into a breach of collective integrity, makes women invisible, and constricts the flow of evidence" (1991, 11). Bert G. Fragner's *Persische Memoirenliteratur als Quelle zur neueren Gescichte Irans* stresses the existence of mechanisms by which authors of Persian memoirs distance themselves from detailed descriptions of their own lives (1979, 5).

Michel Foucault's words made Western man into a "confessing animal." Foucault's formulation in *History of Sexuality* offers useful insights for understanding the differences the critics of Persian literature have pinpointed: "For a long time, the individual was vouched for by the reference of others and the demonstration of his ties to the commonweal (family, allegiance, protection); then he was authenticated by the discourse of truth he was able or obliged to pronounce concerning himself. The truthful confession was inscribed at the heart of the procedures of individualization by power" (1990, 58–59). This inextricable link between discourses of power and subjectivity inform more recent critiques of the very definitions of the genre of autobiography. Not surprisingly, feminists have been at the forefront of such critiques. Echoing Foucault, Sidonie Smith, for instance, writes: "autobiographical storytelling emerged as one powerful means of constituting bourgeois subjects and thereby regulating both bodies and selves" (1998, 10). In "Resisting Autobiography" Caren Kaplan questions the critical tradition that provided us with definitions of autobiography: "Although genre criticism frequently consists of continual definition and redefinition, most autobiography criticism appears to be engaged in a vigorous effort to stabilize and fix generic boundaries" (1992, 117). James Olney, whose works have been in the past cited as instrumental to defining the genre, best sums up the problems with which recent criticism on autobiography has grappled: "Although I have in the past written frequently about autobiography as a literary genre, I have never been very comfortable doing it, primarily because I believe that if one is to speak relevantly of a genre one has first of all to define it, and I have never met a definition of autobiography that I could really like" (1998, xv). In *Memory and Narrative,* from which I have just quoted, Olney proposes the term "pre-autobiography." Others like Caren Kaplan pose challenges of a different nature: "Outlaw genres challenge Western critical practices to expand their parameters and, consequently, shift the subject of autobiography from the individual to a more unstable collective entity" (1992, 134). Kaplan's notion of outlaw genres has interesting potential for reading Persian texts, especially if we accept that a process of individuation similar to the post-Enlightenment construction of subjectivity cannot be traced in Persian letters. This admission does not imply that other discourses of power have not been present in the construction of the collectively minded self we do find in the political memoirs, histories, and travelogues written by Persians.

If we set aside the term "autobiography" in favor of "memoir," we might adopt Roy Pascal's distinction between autobiography and memoir in the author's intention: "In the autobiography proper, attention is focused on the self, in the memoir or reminiscence on others. It is natural, therefore, that autobiographies of statesmen and politicians are almost always in essence memoirs" (1960, 5–6). But, as George Egerton points out even political memoirs resist neat definitions. He argues that "political memoir could best be comprehended as a polygenre—a literary amalgam of diffuse elements of recording, autobiography, biography, political analysis and contemporary historiography" (1994, 23). He concludes, however, that political memoir "finds its most apposite critical location within the broad camp of historiography" (1994, 348). In a similar vein, Ahmad Ashraf finds that Persian memoirs are located within the domain of historiography (1996, 529).

We face yet another problem of definition in discussions of Persian travel literature. In an unpublished piece, Hanaway makes the following distinction between Western and Persian travel writing:

When we think of Western travel narratives, we have in mind mostly those written in the post-Enlightenment period. Modern interpreters of these narratives hold that voluntary travel (as opposed to the official travel engaged in by nineteenth-century Persians) offered the individual an opportunity for expanded experience, which could be interpreted and integrated into the traveler's sense of self. The result of this process could be a change in the understanding of one's self and the world, and it is in this sense that eighteenth—and nineteenth-century travel accounts by Westerners can be thought of as a sub-category of autobiography. The situation of the nineteenth-century Persian travelers is quite different and cannot properly be described using European travel accounts as models. Until the twentieth century when Persian sensibility changed under the influence of European

Romanticism, Persian travel accounts remained quite strictly dynamic and utilitarian. (1)

Other points of distinction could also be found between the Western and the Persian genre of travel literature. As Percy Adams has demonstrated, the evolution of the genre of travel literature in the West is closely linked with the emergence of the novel. Although the beginnings of modern Persian prose are traced to two texts of travel literature, *The Travel Diary of Ibrahim Beg,* the three volumes of which were published during the first decade of the twentieth century, and the Persian translation of James Morier's *Hajji Baba of Ispahan* (Kamshad 1966, 17–27), exact correlations of the type Adams identifies in the Western genres do not necessarily exist in Persian prose fiction.

The long detour I have taken to discuss the genres of autobiography, memoir, political memoir, and travelogue has far from resolved the dilemmas we continue to face in finding correspondences between Persian and European models. This absence of correlation is, in my view, an excellent point of departure. I begin by asking what will be lost if we abandon the Western criteria? Conversely, what might we find by assuming that Persian life writing occurs at the intersections of social history, political memoir, travelogues, and diaries? As many historians and critics of Persian literature have pointed out, writing about the self is always irrevocably bound to the communal and the political. But this notion of the self has not remained static throughout Persian history. If the changes have, in fact, resulted from encounters with other languages, cultures, and histories, can these transmutations not tell us something about the conscious and unconscious adaptations that make up the history of Persian culture?

We know, for instance, that modern Persian literature drew upon Western paradigms. In *Paydayish-i Roman-i Farsi,* Christophe Balaÿ provides a systematic study of the role of literary translation in the formation of the modern Persian novel. The introduction of journalism, new schools modeled on European institutions, and translations all helped to revolutionize Persian political, cultural, and literary systems. Of the educational reforms of the nineteenth century, Hasan Kamshad writes: "under the supervision of European teachers, a great number of celebrated political leaders of the forthcoming years were trained, and many technical and scientific books were either adapted or directly translated from European sources. Meanwhile for the first time a number of Persian students were sent abroad on government scholarships, bringing back with them Western ideas that undoubtedly had a substantial effect on the literary revival in Persia" (1966, 12). This type of interaction not only shaped modern Persian literary production, but, as Hamid Dabashi has noted, it also affected the very nature of Persian language: "The translation movement was crucial in the gradual formation of a simple and deliberately democratic language" (1985, 165).

More nuanced readings of the manner in which aspects of Western civilization filtered through Persian cultural institutions would help us shift the focus away from the Western sources to the transformations to which they were submitted by Persians. In this venture, it might be useful to think in terms of the "arts of contact zone," advocated by Mary Louise Pratt in *Imperial Eyes*.

> I use [contact zone] to refer to the space of colonial encounters, the space in which peoples geographically and historically separated come into contact with each other and establish ongoing relations, usually involving conditions of coercion, radical inequality, and intractable conflict . . . By using the term "contact," I aim to foreground the interactive, improvisational dimensions of colonial encounters so easily ignored or suppressed by diffusionist accounts of conquest and domination. A "contact" perspective emphasizes how subjects are constituted in and by their relations to each other. (1992, 6–7)

What I find particularly interesting in Pratt's vision is the articulation of complex intercultural negotiations and adaptations of the kind I discern in Persian encounters with the West. Even when Persian travelers did not have access to the languages they encountered on their journeys, they endowed themselves with an agency capable of affecting the perception of the other. In other instances, they engaged actively in transmuting other cultures and languages for consumption at home. In this simultaneous metamorphosis of the self and the other I wish to highlight the zones of contact between Persia and its others. In the process, I hope to also demonstrate that the speaking subjects in these narratives of encounter lay bare self-understandings that can shed light on the different configurations of the Persian self in a historical continuum from the premodern to the initiation into modernity. The aloofness of the seventeenth—and nineteenth-century narrators give way to conflictual and paradoxical placements of the self in the narrative of a modern nation. Listening to the voices that speak different, and even contradictory "truths of self" constitutes a first step toward breaking out of the monotony to which many Persian "outlaw genres" have been relegated. This is not to say that some of the texts I have selected have not been studied by historians and literary critics in the past. My own readings build upon existing interpretations, but I do allow myself a certain latitude in creating a "contact zone" between the disciplines that have worked on the same sources I will use in this study. I hope that we find a convergence of interest in discussing the fascinating and, at times unsettling, chapters in the history of Persian culture. The encounters between Persia and other cultures have not always produced salutary results. As I continue to use the term Persia, instead of Iran, I am reminded of one such example.

"Iran" is the word natives of the country use to refer to themselves. But the name by which Europeans used to refer to the country changed in 1935 at the behest of the German ambassador to Tehran. In Ehsan Yarshater's words:

It is said that some German friends of the ambassador persuaded him that, as with the advent of Reza Shah Persia had turned a new leaf in its history and had freed itself from the pernicious influences of Britain and Russia, whose interventions in Persian affairs had practically crippled the country under the Qajars, it was only fitting that the country be called by its own name, "Iran." This would not only signal a new beginning and bring home to the world the new era in Persian history, but would also signify the Aryan race of its population, as "Iran" is a cognate of "Aryan" and derived from it. (1989, 62)

Miron Rezun's *The Iranian Crisis of 1941* further confirms the extent to which the history of this change is linked to the spread of Nazi propaganda in Persia: "To impress the Iranians, a special decree had been issued by the Reich Cabinet as early as 1936 by which the Iranians were exempted from the restrictions of the Nuremberg Racial Laws as pure-blooded Aryans . . . The Iranians were recognized by the Germans as having profound non-Islamic traditions, as distinct from the general Arab-Islamic culture of the New East" (1982, 28–29).

The strictures placed on the use of "Persia" instead of "Iran" were eventually relaxed: "In 1956 the Iranian Government announced that it was no longer prohibited for foreigners to call the country Persia; either Iran or Persia was equally permitted" (Avery 1965, 469). That particular chapter of cultural history had long been closed, although remnants of that era continue to haunt Persian discourses of identity that sometimes blindly eradicate the multiplicity of languages and ethnicities in search of a mythical pure Persian or Iranian culture and identity.

I am aware that in the wake of the 1979 revolution, many of my transplanted compatriots prefer to refer to themselves as Persian instead of Iranian in an attempt to distance themselves from the anti-Iranian sentiments that reek of a bigotry no less forgivable than the racist beliefs Persians promulgated during the reign of Reza Shah. My choice of the word Persia is not informed by this unhappy occasion in our history of cross-cultural encounters. All but one of the texts I analyze were written when Iran was still Persia in the Western imagination. By far the most decisive factor for me was an elegantly composed letter I received from Ehsan Yarshater, who urged me to remember with him the history he had witnessed. That eloquent request, along with my own commitment to understand, if not always accept, the highs and lows of Persian cultural history, made me settle for Persia in my attempt to bring to light some of the complexities that have gone missing from Persian discourses of identity. The fictions of identity I and other Persians have created for ourselves may not have always replicated a spirit of mutual understanding and syncretism, but, in all their complex and varied manifestations, they tell us much about our ways of seeing and comprehending ourselves vis-à-vis others.

1

A Conversion Gone Awry

A narrative of conversion and cultural transplantation, *Don Juan of Persia: A Shi'ah Catholic 1560–1604,* or *Relaciones de Don Juan de Persia,* is the 1604 Spanish text on which the English translation is based. The enigmatic text has its origins in the travel diary kept by Uruch Beg, a secretary attached to a delegation sent by Safavid King, Shah 'Abbas I, to Europe in 1599. As the narrator informs us, the diary, written in Persian, was intended to be delivered to the Persian monarch upon the embassy's return: "From the first moment when I set out from Isfahan on my journey, I diligently carried out the intention I had made to write down carefully all I saw, in order to give an account thereof later to the King of Persia" (Le Strange 1973, 274). But Uruch Beg, following in the footsteps of a few other of his compatriots, converted to Catholicism in Spain and never returned to Persia. Like its author, the diary underwent a metamorphosis. It was translated into Castilian with the help of the Licentiate Alfonso Remón, and the new version, including a descriptive history and geography of Persia, was presented to the Spanish king, Philip III.

Uruch Beg's conversion made him an embarrassment to the Persian ambassador, whose own nephew, also a part of the embassy, had embraced Catholicism before Uruch Beg: "So strongly were Husain 'Ali Beg's feelings aroused over this conversion that he attempted to have Don Juan (Uruch Beg) murdered" (Lockhart 1997, 387). The ambassador's attempt to do away with Don Juan can be seen as an act of self-preservation in comparison with other envoys of the Safavid era who "committed suicide before returning to Iran for fear of the shah's wrath at having failed their mandates" (Mathee 1998, 242). Uruch Beg survived the attempt on his life, but he was not destined to live long.

Within a year of the publication of *Relaciones de Don Juan de Persia* Uruch Beg/Don Juan was accidentally killed. The following account of Don Juan's end is related by Le Strange in his introduction to *Don Juan of Persia*: "On the 15th of May of 1605, when still resident in Valladolid, he was involved in a scuffle with the men attending a law officer, an Alcalde de Corte, and in the brawl he came to be stabbed, cut down and killed. To spare embarrassing questions his body was then and there flung into a desolate gully near the capital, where, as reported, it was eaten by town dogs" (1973, 10). The manner of disposal of the body implies that even as Don Juan, Uruch Beg could not be saved from his status as a renegade. The Spaniards who rejoiced in his conversion continued to remember him as Don Juan *of* Persia, forever locking him in a hyphenated existence aptly noted in the subtitle of Le Strange's English translation, *A Shi'ah Catholic.*

The unknown whereabouts of Uruch Beg's original Persian diary, noted by Mohamad Tavakoli-Targhi (1990, 74), and its adaptation into Spanish have relegated the only record, albeit altered, we have of this convert's life to a marginal status. For instance, Rudi Mathee mentions Uruch Beg's travelogue as a rare instance of Persian writings about the West under Safavid rule, but he concludes that "having adopted Christianity, [Uruch Beg] never intended to return to Iran and his writings were therefore not aimed at an Iranian readership" (1998, 242). To add to the ambiguities of the narrative of Don Juan's life, there is a passage in which the narrator speaks of a plan to keep his conversion hidden from the Persian ambassador in order to be able to return to Persia. The return journey, we are told, was to enable him to bring back with him his wife and son. But the duke of Lerma, to whom the Persian presented his plans, is said to have reminded Don Juan that he had chosen the love of God over the love of wife and son. More importantly, the duke spoke to Don Juan about the risks inherent in executing his idea of traveling to Persia incognito. As we know, the Persian ambassador discovered Don Juan's secret, further undermining any plans of return.

In addition to the problems of intended readership signaled by Mathee, little value can be gained by reading *Don Juan of Persia* as a historical document. There is, however, merit in uncovering the ambiguities of a text that claims to speak for the Persian whose own voice has been long lost and in deciphering through those very ambiguities the compelling forces that led Uruch Beg to shift his allegiances from one center of power to another. If I de-emphasize Uruch Beg's, or for that matter Don Juan's, individuality, it is because both Persian and Spanish subjects were constructed along different axes at that time. Not only did collective identity take precedence over that of the individual, the collectivity itself was defined in relation to the figure of the monarch and the religious and political power he embodied. The discourses of identity to which Uruch Beg and Don Juan were subject are manifest in the incongruous voices that emerge from a narrative that was itself required to comply with Spanish cultural expectations.

The Spanish translator and editor, Remón, demonstrates an eagerness to create a text that would conform to the literary expectations of the elite audience of the times. Sonnets written to Don Juan by Spanish Golden Age literati accompanied the edition Remón produced. Alonso Cortés notes in the 1946 edition of *Relaciones de Don Juan de Persia*: "As can be seen, among the poets who here praised Don Juan of Persia figure talents as famous as Doctor Maximiliano de Céspedes, a great friend of Lope de Vega, Doctor Augustín de Tejada y Páez, collaborator with Espinosa in *Flores,* and Alonso de Ledesma, the famous author of *Spiritual Concepts*" (1946, 45–46).[1] Remón went further by appending a poem to the text that he claimed to have been authored by Don Juan. These poetic appendages point to a desire to make Don Juan's narrative fit within the cultural and literary norms of seventeenth-century Spain.

In his poem Alonso de Ledesma describes Don Juan as Persia's new Apollo, "A Homer of the history in which he was Mars, / since his sword is equal to his pen" (Alonso Cortés 1946, 51), elevating him to a nobility parallel to that of the Spanish courtiers. Maximiliano de Céspedes's sonnet echoes

---

1. For translations from this Spanish edition I am indebted to George Lang, who also consulted with Richard Young, a colleague with expertise in the literature of Spanish Golden Age.

a similar sentiment, commemorating Don Juan's successful melding of his heritage and his new identity: "To be truly Spanish while Persian / to imitate the nobility of mantle" (1946, 46). These sonnets combine a reverence for the convert with an acknowledgment of the inexorable differences that embracing Catholicism cannot eradicate. At best Don Juan aspires to emulate the cultural ethos of the Spanish elite.

If Uruch Beg could never fully become Don Juan, the translation of the diary he had intended for the king of Persia also failed at erasing traces of its author's earlier affiliations. The ambivalences we glean from the narrative communicate something of an anxiety that haunts this inadvertent transcultural journey. Although the version of the text we have received was meant to transmit an enthusiasm for the happy accident that enabled Uruch Beg to become a Catholic and remain in Spain, it does not represent leaving Persia as a cherished first step. On the contrary, the description of the embassy's departure is imbued with a sense of foreboding: "Diverse were the feelings in the hearts of those who were thus departing, and different their expression: for some set forth most joyfully, but others very dolefully. To all the king had graciously given his royal word to bestow on us at our return many favors, but such were the tears of our relatives, the sad faces shown by our friends, the sorrow and despair expressed differently but grievously by wives, fathers, children, that we had perforce at last hurriedly to conclude and depart" (Le Strange 1973, 234–35). The same part of the narrative marks the introduction of a physical *and* symbolic distance separating the members of the embassy and their well-wishers gathered on the shore of the Caspian: "Now many of our friends and relations had come out accompanying us hither on the road from Isfahan, and when we had at last embarked in our ship very sorrowfully we bade them good-bye, we standing on board, and finally set sail" (235). After a stormy day at sea, the Persians are surprised to discover that they have returned to the same shoreline they thought to have already left the day before. The storm and concerns about the difficult journeys ahead makes some Persians long to return to the firm ground of their homeland—a thought they are forced to banish from their minds because "we all feared too much the wrath of Shah 'Abbas" (237).

The Persians' lack of familiarity with seafaring was probably at the root of their readiness to forsake the mission, but other factors contributed to their reluctance to embark on a voyage away from their well-grounded sense of identity. As Rudi Mathee states: "The Iranian perception of the surrounding world as articulated in Safavid chronicles . . . suggests an Iranocentric world view. Safavid chronicles evoke a universe with Iran at its center and present a realm ruled by a monarch who was seen as God's viceregent and, as grandiosely, the exalted sovereign of the world" (1998, 241). Mathee also points to a "conviction that foreigners naturally stood in awe of Iran's great past and needed Iran more than the country needed them" (243).[2]

This era in Persian history is characterized by successful attempts to carve out a consolidated political identity: "to the Safawis belongs the credit of making Persia, after the lapse of eight centuries and a half, 'a nation once again' " (Browne 1959, 12). The ruling dynasty, the Safavids, arrived at this political sovereignty through the construction of a religiously unified community of Shi'ites with an identity distinct from other Islamic dominions. What the Safavids seized on, as Roger Savory points out, was the political and ideological dimension of the history of Shi'ism:

Shi'ism was, in origin, a political movement, the Shi'at 'Ali (Party of 'Ali), which supported the claim to the Caliphate of 'Ali, the cousin and son-in-law of the Prophet Muhammad. Shi'is believe that Muhammad formally designated 'Ali as his successor *(kalifa)* at a ceremony at Ghadir khumm in the year 632. Shi'is therefore regard the first three caliphs (Abu Bakr, 'Umar and 'Uthman) as usurpers, and the ritual cursing of these persons has always been the proper duty of Shi'is, although the emphasis placed on it varied from time to time. In the early days of the Safavid state, when revolutionary fervour was still strong, great emphasis was placed on this ritual cursing. (1980, 27)

2. In his analysis of Safavid history and historiography, Roger Savory also points to the increased wealth of the country, through the enhancement of trade and traditional industries, as sources of self-sufficiency at this time (1995, 279).

To achieve the unification of Persia under the banner of Shi'ism, the Safavids invoked a myth intertwining pre-Islamic Persian history and the beginnings of the Islamic era. In Savory's words, they "assert[ed] that 'Ali's younger son, Husayn, married the daughter of Yazdigird III, the last of the Sasanid kings," thereby linking "the family of 'Ali with the ancient Iranian monarchical tradition, and the divine right of the Iranian kings" (Savory 1980, 27). The creation and propagation of the discourses of Persian identity during the Safavid era converge with their political aim of preserving the territories of Persia from the neighboring Ottoman Empire.[3] It is against this background that the mission of which Uruch Beg was a member was dispatched to Europe.

In keeping with the Safavid lack of interest in Europe, the very idea for the embassy was initiated by an Englishman, Sir Anthony Sherley, who, though without proper credentials, passed himself off as capable of promoting the interest of the Persian king and European rulers against their common enemy, the Ottoman Empire. Don Juan's narrative speaks of "the timely arrival of certain Englishmen" (Le Strange 1973, 227) and the effect they had on Shah 'Abbas: "[Sir Anthony Sherley] gave himself out as cousin of the Scottish king James, saying that all the kings of Christendom had recognized him as such, and had empowered him as their ambassador to treat with the king of Persia, who should make a confederacy with them in order to wage war against the Turk, who was indeed the common enemy of all of them" (232). Don Juan does not give a particularly flattering image of Sir Anthony, whom he blames for the disappearance of gifts the Persians had brought for European dignitaries: "It now appeared that the whole affair had been a cheat, for no chests had ever been brought to Rome, Sir Anthony having sold or bartered away their contents" (284). Lost with the precious cargo was the Persians' trust in Sir Anthony and, by extension, in the exaggerated claims he had made to the

---

3. Interestingly the Safavid attempts at unifying Persia did not extend to the realm of language. The court itself practiced linguistic diversity. Numerous scholars have written about the literary and administrative languages of the Safavid era. Among them Browne, in the fourth volume of *The Literary History of Persia*, Roger Savory, in *Iran under Safavids*, Ehsan Yarshater, in "The Indian or Safavid Style" (1988), and John Perry, in "Persian in the Safavid Period" (1996).

Persian monarch. It is interesting to note that the narrator's contempt stems from the Englishman's betrayal of the Persian king, hinting at competing allegiances that resurface in other segments of the text. Even the narrator's decision to convert to Catholicism and his feelings toward his new faith become entrapped in incongruities that appear to subvert Remón's efforts in infusing the text with an adequate sense of the recent convert's disdain for his former beliefs and his passion for Catholicism.

We gain a glimpse of Remón's role as translator and editor in Guy Le Strange's introduction to his English translation. In a letter prefixed to the Castilian text, Le Strange tells us, Remón presents himself as "an intimate friend of Don Juan's" (1973, 10). Le Strange goes on to sum up Remón's letter: "Remón, after praising his new friend, as a man well educated in accordance with eastern standards, stating further that his knowledge of the history and geography of Persia was astonishingly profound, continues that he, Remón, had recently been helping Don Juan to compose in Castilian the work following, translating it page by page from the original draft which Don Juan had written out in Persian" (10–11).

As Le Strange indicates, Uruch Beg's knowledge of Spanish would not have been very sophisticated, although a Spanish priest named Don Francisco Guasque, canon of Barcelona, was appointed to accompany the convert and to instruct him in matters of language and faith. We also find out in Uruch Beg's narrative that, even after his decision to embrace Christianity, he had to approach Spanish through the Persian alphabet: "In the Persian script and language, even as before had been the case with my Diary, I now constrained my hand to write down the prayers, the articles of belief, the Commandments, and other Christian ordinances that were necessary for instructing one like me, an infidel, who was about to become a catechumen" (299). This imbuing of Persian script with Catholic and Spanish import marks an act of both translation and transgression, not unlike the process through which Remón made the Persian diary over into a Spanish text. One language is apparently emptied out of its cultural specificity in order to take on new, altered meaning. Similarly, Uruch Beg's Persian text has to lose its original intent and significance to be received by Spanish readers. Encapsulated in this statement about Uruch

Beg's way of learning Spanish is an important insight into this narrative of conversion: its position at linguistic and cultural crossroads. In spite of the tone of humility vis-à-vis his newly adopted faith, the Persian convert also hints at a painful and slow process through which he struggled to transform his linguistic and cultural affiliations. As Don Juan "constrains" his hand to make the Persian alphabet convey Spanish, Remón seems to have striven to make the Persian adopt a different authorial voice. But that voice is riddled with paradoxes.

Chapter 1 of Don Juan's narrative begins with the following passage marking an interesting shift of pronouns from "we" to "I":

> We shall have a succinct but exact description of our country as it is at the present time, setting down the native Persian names, which may thus be compared and adjusted to those given by ancient and modern authorities who have written or shall in the future write from hearsay. For indeed in this matter I speak as an eye-witness, and therefore, if in the works of Thomas Minadoi or Giovanni Botero any diversity of names be found from what I shall here set down, the reader must know that mine are the real Persian names, as spoken in the native tongue of my country, while theirs are but mistaken versions, being, in fact, misunderstood or wrongly pronounced words. (36)

Don Juan's authority having thus been established, it is then put to the test in the opening sentence of chapter 2. The beginning of the historical and geographical overview, for example, reads: "According to Strabo, Persia is the country south of Parthia and Carmania, between the provinces of Media on the west and Hircania on the east, having—if we are to believe Peter Apianus—Arabia to the South of the same" (38). This first sentence subordinates the native knowledge invoked in chapter 1 to the existing Western documents on Persia. Revealed here is Don Juan's function as a native informant in bolstering Europe's narratives of discovery. He represents an authority who can correct and surpass the archives of Western knowledge on Persia. In other words, the narrative voice has to negotiate a balance between a necessary identification with Europeans and an equally authoritative position vis-à-vis Persia.

This balancing act repeats itself in chapter 3 of the first book, which opens with an admission of the necessity of providing detailed presentation of Persia's manner and form of government: "The method of government of the Persian kings being peculiar, we shall treat of the affairs of this kingdom in some detail in order to make the matter perfectly clear" (45). But by the time we reach book 2, this need for comprehensive explanations has to be counterbalanced with an identification with Europe. In a description of the Persian court's complex relations to various tribal powers, we read: "But I need not explain further these matters of state, and should be speaking prolixly, for wars in Persia are waged very differently to what we have any knowledge of in Spain, and there all things are alien to the politics of our western lands" (201). This type of identification with the European perspective is, at other times, abandoned.

One such instance appears in an episode in which Don Juan relates how in a battle he lost his father. Here the chronicle intersects with personal history and the voice no longer belongs to a chronicler identifying with Europeans for whom he is writing, but rather is that of a son mourning the cruel fate suffered by his father:

> Protesting and against my will they carried me before the king, who praised and sought to give me comfort, but I was in that state when all reason fails: and yet the more so when I came to see that from the wall of the fortress the Turks were exhibiting, stuck on a lance point, my poor father's head, thus further to insult and humiliate me, for his body in their brutal rage they had already burnt. The king and prince both did great honour to the memory of my father by what manner they spoke of him to me, and they made me a promise of future favour. (192–93)

Although the narrator is now a Catholic who, in other parts of his narrative, disparages the religious practices of his Shi'ite compatriots, in evoking the memory of his father, he revels in the recollection of how the Shah ordered a picture of his father to be painted and be "placed above the door of one of the Mosques of Tabriz, that is dedicated to the honour of the great Amir Haydar, the father of Shah Ismail, who is held by us Persians to have been a saint" (193). There is no hesitation here to identify with the Persians from whom the narrative voice, on more than one occasion, will attempt to dissociate Uruch Beg. The memory of the desecration of his father's body evokes such pain that the narrator abandons all pretense of adherence to Catholic propriety.

The narrative also bears traces of Persian stereotypes of cultures just beyond the borders of Persia. The expedition made by the embassy across Russia is described at certain moments from a position of apparent cultural superiority. The first Christian town they stop in is Kazan, which the narrator depicts as "extremely full of churches, each having many great bells, and on the vesper of feast days no one can sleep or indeed stay in the city for the noise" (243). In the narrator's imagination, life in Kazan represents many extremes of which the overabundance of churches and their bells' noisy protestations of faith are only a few. Among other aspects of life in Kazan the narrator remarks: "What they lack is good wine, and they have only one kind of drink, which is made from wheat or barley, and this is so strong that those who drink it are often drunk. For this reason there is a law and ordinance that no officer may carry any kind of weapon, otherwise they would be killing each other every other moment" (244). Albeit understated, the narrative tone is infused with righteousness. A much stronger sense of moral disapproval is evident in the passages devoted to the embassy's stay in Nizhni: "The people of Nizhni are Christians, and subjects of the Duke of Muscovy; but they are of a lascivious habit, and the fame of the place lies in its bath-houses, where the men and the women are wont to bathe in company, promiscuously, with no clothes to cover their nakedness; hence their commerce is exceedingly free, more so indeed than in any other country would be tolerated as possible" (247). This passage marks an anxiety about open interactions between the sexes and the fear that it would lead to moral degeneration. As Tavakoli-Targhi indicates in "Imagining Western Women," this kind of concern was to dominate Persian travel narratives of the eighteenth and nineteenth centuries (1993, 73–87).

Don Juan's narrative provides only occasional references to women and their appearance. Russian women in particular become embodiments of shortcomings of both culture and nature. In a passage about the town of Vladimir, the narrator notes: "The women here are extremely beautiful, but their mode of dress is so ugly and eccentric, and they display so little taste for a suitable combination of colours, that their clothes do not favour them" (249). The homeliness remarked here eventually extends to the surfeit of pomp and power the embassy witnesses in its audience with the duke of Muscovy. Although the exercise of absolute power was not unfamiliar to the Persian subjects, the person of the duke comes in for harsh criticism:

> The Grand Duke is extremely rich, for he is lord of both the lives and goods of all his subjects, to do therewith at his will; and they all serve and worship him. He allows no schools or universities in his kingdom, in order—as he says—that no one may come to know all that he himself knows; and hence no one of his presidents, governors and secretaries of state can know more than what the Grand Duke wishes him to know of his affairs. No one is allowed to call in any physician, who is a foreigner, to cure him; and no one, under pain of death, may leave Muscovy to go into any foreign country, lest he should get into communication with other folk and learn better. (252–53)

The intertwining of power and knowledge is reinforced later in the same passage: "There are no books other than the Gospels and Lives of Saints, and all the people go hung about with crosses" (253). The presentation of the power wielded by the duke of Muscovy emphasizes a lack of subtlety and culture that might have originated in the Persian views of Russians: "Of all non-Muslim major peoples, none were held in lower esteem than the Russians. Just as Russia was not included in the contemporaneous Western European idea of the community of civilized nations, so it had never fallen under the generic rubric of Farang in the Islamic world, including Iran . . . In keeping with long-standing views in the Islamic world at large, the Iranians thought the Russians to be the 'most base and the most infamous of all Christians' and the 'Uzbegs of Europe' " (Mathee 1998, 233).

The descriptions of encounters with races who could not be readily categorized according to existing norms of identification lay bare attempts at creating convergences of European and Persian perspectives. The depiction of people of the Arctic is an interesting case in point: "The men and the women are both of one appearance in the face, the men having neither beards nor eyebrows; further, they are of very short stature, so that if any people may be named in truth the Pygmies, they are the [Lapps]. They are smaller even than any of the dwarfs that we have in Spain. . . . The eyes of these men are so small that scarcely can they see out of them" (263). This passage is a remarkable example of an attempt to pinpoint alterity across multiple archives of knowledge. Ultimately, the encoding of racial difference resorts to a cataloging of the "unusual" and the "freakish" in nature. What begins with the classification of visible differences becomes integrated into an examination of the self in the mirror of the other that culminates in a process of cultural conversion.

Sartorial differences, for instance, become the focus of much commentary and they begin to be noted for their function in the construction of religious and political identity. As Marjorie Garber notes, dress codes were means of controlling and disciplining the social body: "All over Europe in the medieval and early modern periods sumptuary laws were promulgated by cities, towns, and nation states, to regulate who wore what, and on what occasion. The term 'sumptuary' is related to 'consumption'; the laws were designed in part to regulate commerce and to support local industries, as well as prevent—or at least to hold to a minimum—what today would be known as 'conspicuous consumption,' the flaunting of wealth by those whose class or other social designation made such display seem transgressive" (1992, 21). Although it did not fit within the type of transgression described by Garber, the Persians witnessed a deliberate act of concealment of identity through dress just before their arrival in Stade: "And now, in the sight of us all, our Franciscan Friar dressed himself in Persian clothes, for this place is wholly inhabited by Lutherans, and Sir Anthony had assured him that should it become known as how he was by religion a Papist, infallibly they would tear him to pieces" (Le Strange 1973, 265). Seeing the Franciscan friar dressed as a Persian is a foreshadowing of the manner in which the Persians will try out European attire as a means of donning a new identity. From this point on, the relationship between clothes and identity becomes increasingly more noticeable in the diary. Also noteworthy is the new gaze the narrator/observer adopts vis-à-vis Europe and Europeans. Moreover, the narrator is now conscious of the fact that he too is being observed and his gaze is being returned. The narrative voice no longer merely records differing appearances and customs, but rather becomes implicated in the very curiosities being catalogued. For example, in the chapter pertaining to the embassy's arrival in Valladolid, where Don Juan's journey comes to an end, there is a reference to how the Persian was regarded by the locals: "On entering Valladolid, the novelty of my Persian dress caused such astonishment, that quite a multitude followed after me through the streets" (289). This exchange of gazes is preceded by other challenges to Persian received knowledge. In a tour the Persians are given of the city of Embden, German and Persian claims to truth, mediated via the Spanish commentator, enter into a field of contestation:

> But they showed us, among other matters, a storage-house for wheat, so huge, with so many separate granaries, and these so full of corn, that we were assured there was a supply here to last ninety years. This we could scarce credit, but they insisted so much on it, that we ended by believing them. But this wheat of theirs has in it no heart, and is all husk, and the grain is longer than it is in Spanish wheat; on the other hand, in substance it is heavier than the grains of our oats, being less than the weight of rye. This sort of wheat we too have in Persia, and the Persians know it by the name of *Chaudar*. (267)

Instead of the Persians' own observations it is the obstinacy of their tour guides that forces them to acquiesce to the Germans' claim to truth. Even the additional information brought to bear by the Spanish editor does not diminish the element of disbelief initially registered. If the Persians feign acceptance, it is with the understanding that their knowledge, however incontestable it might be, is not going to be acknowledged by the residents of Embden. The citing of the Persian name for the particular type of wheat underlines the Persian visitors' clinging to their own beliefs, but implicit in this need to invoke terms native to Persia is recognition that those frames of reference are gradually losing their leverage.

That the Persian norms and expectations are increasingly less operative is graphically represented in the description of a dinner the embassy attends in Kassel: "On the very first day, when we dined with the Prince, the loaves of bread, the napkins, knives and salt-cellars that stood on the table, all were made of sugar, as also the various kinds of fruit. And in every case each item exactly resembled and imitated the form and texture of the object it simulated. Great was the laughter when we tried to cut some fruit with these knives, which, of course, crumbled and went to pieces in our hands" (269). This crumbling is emblematic of the process some members of the embassy are beginning to undergo. From the dissimulation in Embden to the simulations in Kassel, the narrative of the journey reveals an increasing recognition of alterity as a means of access to other forms of power. Whatever impact these subtle reminders might have had on the Persian travelers, they were offered an unequivocal invitation to embrace difference by none other than the pope himself.

The narrator presents this description of the Persians' audience with the pope: "His Holiness then gave us his blessing, saying, 'May God make you Christians' " (285). In spite of the gloss given to the narrative after the fact, the conversions are not solely inspired by the Persians' sudden and miraculous religious illumination. At the very least, religion has to be seen as standing in for a gamut of cultural markers by which the Persians' curiosity was provoked. An examination of the events preceding the various conversions, including Uruch Beg's own, provides the rough outlines of other equally compelling forces drawing the Persians toward new self-configurations.

Of the first three converts and the process by which they arrived at their decision we learn little. Their resolution to embrace Christianity seems to have been made shortly after the audience with the pope:

> Thus we left Rome without the Englishmen, and next, when we had gone
> forth we perceived that three of our fellow Persians too were wanting. We

therefore went back to find them, and discovered that already God had begun the work of His divine Grace. For these three Persians who had now left us we found in the palace of his Holiness in Rome, and they were studying to become Christian converts. The ambassador was thereby much perturbed, and seeking audience of the Pope, his Holiness answered him that the Divine Law was indeed one of kindness, that none by force was brought to believe, that all were free to act as they would, and that what he, the Pope, was doing was done in accordance with God's will. On this the ambassador spoke to the three men apart, and finding them steadfast and firm of purpose to become Christians, left them. (286–87)

The ambassador's willingness to leave the Persians behind might have been in part due to their station in life. Le Strange states in a footnote accompanying this segment of the narrative that "The three converts were the barber, the cook and a certain private secretary; not, however, one of the four official Secretaries of the Embassy . . . three of whom later joined the Roman Communion in Spain" (337). That the conversion process was facilitated with a guarantee of income is preserved in historical records and is cited by Le Strange: " 'the Pope is to give them ten crowns monthly, and he is in hopes that the King of Persia may likewise abandon the Mussulman Faith' " (337).

The next Persian to choose the same path is the ambassador's nephew. Because of the impact and magnitude of his actions, we receive a far more detailed account of the event:

In the midst of these festivities a matter was happening which was to cause much disquietude to our ambassador. Among his secretaries of Embassy who had accompanied him from Persia, being of his suite, was his nephew, whose name was 'Ali Quli Beg, and he, because the subject pleased and interested him, was now wont to attend the rites and services of the Christian church. He had further come to appreciate the Spanish mode of life, and for convenience was accustomed now to wear the Spanish dress. This at first apparently was done as a matter of mere curiosity and amusement, but in truth it was soon patent that, as we may opine and believe, the hour had struck in which

God Almighty . . . was now intent that in Spain He should be proclaimed
again as God Almighty. (292)

Convenience and curiosity appear to have been the primary incentives for 'Ali
Quli Beg to become a Catholic. Particularly striking is how he moves from his
observation of religious ceremonies, to trying out Spanish outfits, and finally
to wishing to become a Catholic. The undertone of fascination is barely disguised by the rhetoric of salvation later inserted. It is significant that 'Ali Quli
Beg's experiments with identity are punctuated with cross-dressing and per-
forming new rituals. For 'Ali Quli Beg, it would appear, becoming Catholic is
as much about dressing up for the part as about internalizing the articles of
faith. Although this same logic does not necessarily extend to Uruch Beg, it
must nevertheless be acknowledged that the ambassador's nephew played an
important part in instigating Uruch Beg's conversion. Uruch Beg was sent to
Valladolid to give the canon an account of an unfortunate incident in which
the Shi'ite clergyman accompanying the mission was killed in Mérida. Once in
Valladolid, he spoke to 'Ali Quli Beg, and as a result of a conversation with
him and priests at the Jesuit House "it became manifest how God Almighty
willed that a miracle should be worked in me. For I began immediately to feel
an inordinate longing in my heart to seek and find His Divine Grace . . . and
while I was yet a prey to this confusion of mind, and unable to declare clearly
my desire, the Divine Will loosed my slow tongue—even as with Moses of
old—and just as I was returned to my lodging house I urgently called upon
the Fathers to grant me baptism, though no master had yet given me any sufficient instruction in religion" (299). Perhaps the murder of the Persian clergyman exerted its own symbolic power of persuasion on Uruch Beg. His
compatriots' conversions and the murder would have all acted as forceful reminder that the Persians had stepped outside the Persian monarch's realm of
power and, by extension, the community of religious and political belief that
was inextricably bound with the self-understanding of a Persian subject. The
attempt on Don Juan's life was an extension of the disciplining arm of the
monarch. It was also a form of expulsion from the community of Persians who
had, during the journey, stood in for all that he had left behind.

After this episode, the narrator withdraws from the company of his compatriots, couching his banishment as an inevitable outcome of his conversion: "I soon discovered that, being now a Christian, the conversation of my Persian fellow countrymen, with whom I had heretofore been on terms of inseparable comradeship, was now no longer in any sense to my taste" (303). Yet, the unraveling of these ties was not as complete as claimed by the narrator. In fact, even on the final page of the manuscript, as we read of his now being at peace with his life as a Christian among the Spanish, we glimpse something of the convert's continuing longing for his family: "I have now written this Book of mine more with the intent of giving praise to God for His marvellous loving-kindness daily shown to me, than indeed for any merely mundane cause. Let me therefore confess before the Divine Majesty of God, how content I am to be a Christian, and I have at last lost all memory of the natural pain I once felt at finding myself cut off for ever from my wife, my son, my country and all I there possessed" (308). After all the transformations this text has undergone, it reeks of a failed transculturation and leaves a tangible trace of what was lost in the Persian's attempt at religious and cultural conversion. That the narrator should mention the loss of the "natural pain" of longing for his family only underlines its tenacity and force. Not only did Don Juan not succeed in suppressing his homesickness, he did not even secure his personal peace and safety. His remains being cast into a gully is emblematic of this outcast's brief and trying sojourn in Spain.

If little of this anguish and suffering is conveyed in the text handed down to us, it is because what we read of Don Juan's story is a palimpsest, a writing over what is erased in the process of translation and cultural conversion. The manuscript produced by Remón is a deliberate reworking carefully hiding obliterated layers, even if now and then it inadvertently points up evidence of tampering.

The most ironic aspect of this Persian's story is that the embassy of which Uruch Beg was a member left behind a Persia obsessed with defining itself through an enforced religious community only to be confronted with a competing compulsory Catholicism. Ultimately his adopted homeland proved to be no more hospitable than the country of his birth. Perhaps the failure of this transculturation can be best understood in light of the similar socioreligious conditions prevailing in Persia and Spain of that time. In such a climate, a hyphenated existence was a near impossibility. Regardless of his change of name and religious affiliation, Uruch Beg was fated to become a missing Persian.

My own attempt at recovering the lost story of his life does little to reestablish facts. If anything, my infusing hints of personal anguish into this apparently seamless narrative of conversion only draws attention to other possible layers of fiction others might extract from it. Perhaps Don Juan's participation in Remón's imaginative translation is the best indication we have of the need he felt to leave behind a life history of sorts and his understanding that a good deal of that history would forever remain hidden.

Centuries later, we continue to wonder how to read a text that resists categorization into historical chronicle or life history. If the translated narrative cannot be placed among similar Persian chronicles, it cannot be read exclusively as a product of Castilian culture of the Golden Age. Uruch Beg/Don Juan and Remón contributed equally to the creation of a testimonial at the crossroads of seventeenth-century Persian and Spanish cultures, best seen as a phenomenon of "contact zone."

2

The Tribulations of an Early Tourist

Much of the ambiguity and uncertainty surrounding *Don Juan of Persia* can be directly attributed to its being translated and reconfigured by an editor. But one of the effects of the transformation of Uruch Beg's travelogue into a description of Persia is that the narrative is anchored in a sense, however distorted and inaccurate it might be, of Persian history, especially the events preceding the Persian embassy's departure for Europe.

We find no such context and background in the narrative of Haji Mirza Muhammad 'Ali Mu'in al-Saltanah's travels to Europe and North America in 1893, although here too an editor has had a hand in the presentation of text to modern readers. It is indeed difficult to approach this travelogue without passing through the frame surrounding its reprinting in 1982.

The reprinted Persian text is the only form in which I have had access to this travelogue. The questions the editor's introduction to the reprinted version did not answer were crucial in forming my own strategies for reading this narrative.

Mu'in al-Saltanah's record of travels was first published in 1901 by Georges Meunier in Paris. The handwritten manuscript, of which five hundred copies were originally printed, seems to have remained inaccessible in French national archives until 1982, when Humayun Shahidi discovered it and published a year later with a preface and an introduction to the history of Persian-American relations. For Shahidi, the manuscript carries considerable historical weight that he would like to see linked to all other early encounters between Persians and Americans. Shahidi's motives are understandable. A mere three years after a revolution that ruptured relations between Persians and Americans the discovery of an early narrative of travel to the United States would excite the interest of any historian of Persian culture. In pursuit of a better understanding of the history of contacts between the two nations, Shahidi's introduction discusses the history of diplomatic relations between Persia and the United States. Curiously he does not address Mu'in al-Saltanah's place in the gallery of prominent Persians and Americans who were the first to visit one another's countries.

The only comments Shahidi makes about the manuscript pertain to its layout and the original daguerreotypes, reproduced in his edition. All but one of the daguerreotypes are of sites the Persian visited in Europe. The one exception is an image of Mu'in al-Saltanah and the interpreter who accompanied him during the American part of his journey. Shahidi also speaks of certain irregularities in the Persian transliteration of European and American terms and names that he found necessary to adapt to contemporary usage. But even in this aspect of his task as the mediator between the travelogue and its potential readers today Shahidi leaves some questions unanswered. Some words are often spelled differently in various segments of the narrative. Occasionally attempts are made to reproduce the name of a city in its original European or American spelling. In these cases, the results are not much better than in the Persian transliterations, because it is not always clear which European language is being drawn upon for the spelling. It might well be that these insertions appear in the original manuscript and are the product of Mu'in al-Saltanah's own lack of familiarity with the languages in question. If the absence of systematic punctuation in the text, reflecting the standards of Mu'in al-Saltanah's time, is any indication, perhaps the problems of transliteration can also be attributed to the author.

It is also unclear whether the title of the work, *Chicago Travelogue: Haji Mirza Muhammad Ali Mu'in al-Saltanah's Journal of travels to Europe and the United States in 1893,* accompanied the original manuscript. Chicago could easily have been the focal point of the title as Mu'in al-Saltanah's ultimate destination was the World Columbian Exposition of 1893. In the initial part of his journey, he accompanied his father, Haji Aqa Muhammad Muʻin al-Tujjar, to Vienna for an eye operation. They spent "a few months in Vienna" (Muʻin al-Saltanah 1982, 204) and Baden. After his father's return to Persia, Muʻin al-Saltanah joined a friend, Haji Muhammad Baqir Tajir Khurasani, on a trip to Italy. This friend, also a merchant, Muʻin al-Saltanah tells us, was a resident of Vienna, where he probably became fluent in German, and had visited Italy before. It was the friend's prior knowledge of Italy, Muʻin al-Saltanah appears to imply, that prompted and facilitated this part of the journey.

Neither the author nor the editor speaks of any further motivation for the continuation of this journey to the United States, which Muʻin al-Saltanah undertook on his own. Implicit in the narrative is Muʻin al-Saltanah's interest as a merchant in the Exposition. As indicated in his surname, Muʻin al-Tujjar (merchants' advocate), Muʻin al-Saltanah's father's prominent status as a merchant was acknowledged in the title which would have been bestowed upon him by the monarch. His other title, Haji, indicates his having had enough independent economic means to have undertaken a pilgrimage to Mecca.

Muʻin al-Saltanah and his father were obviously wealthy enough to travel to the West, and in the case of Muʻin al-Saltanah, he hoped to come back enriched with goods and information. The official record of the Exposition, *The Book of the Fair*, which might well reflect the propaganda surrounding the Fair, certainly confirms this impression: "If to any class of visitors the Columbian Exposition was somewhat of a disappointment, it was to those who went there merely in search of amusement, but instruction conveyed in its most attractive form, was the main purpose of the Fair, and surely there were never such opportunities for a comparative study of what has and is being accomplished in every branch of industry and art" (Bancroft 1893, 835). Muʻin al-Saltanah could have been lured by the prospect of having in one place a display of advances made in numerous parts of the globe. And he had the financial means to undertake the long journey. As Muʻin al-Saltanah indicates the 1893 journey was not his first outside Persia. He tells us that he visited the Paris Exposition and spent forty days there. Muʻin al-Saltanah's ability to travel to Europe and North America in an unofficial capacity can be tied to his economic and social status and is probably responsible for his apparent lack of interest in meeting heads of state.

There are only two occasions on which Mu'in al-Saltanah either professes an interest in or meets the dignitaries of the countries he visits. The first is during his visit to the Vatican. Without much preamble, he inserts in his descriptions of the Vatican: "I asked whether I could meet the pope. I was told that without the government's permission it is not possible to meet the pope. The government will obviously not issue a permission unless they know the person in question. Therefore, I was not able to meet him" (238–39).[1] The offhand nature of Mu'in al-Saltanah's remarks makes it seem as if his wish for an audience with the pope is an extension of his tour of the churches and the relics. As we shall see in the more extended analysis of this segment of his journey, he is thoroughly fascinated with the institutions of the church. But his curiosity about the person of the pope and his interactions with the political government of Italy are integral to the overall pattern of Mu'in al-Saltanah's curiosity. Because Persian government at this time is closely aligned with the power of Shi'ite clergy, Mu'in al-Saltanah becomes fascinated with a European parallel he believes to detect in the Vatican. To borrow from Michael Taussig's conceptions of mimesis and alterity, it is the logic of sameness that fortifies Mu'in al-Saltanah against his encounters with differences. We shall see scenes described by Mu'in al-Saltanah in which he is caught between "play[ing] this trick of dancing between the very same and the very different," what Taussig sees as part of the process of "all identity formation [which] is engaged in this habitually bracing activity in which the issue is not so much staying the same, but maintaining sameness through alterity" (1993, 129).

Mu'in al-Saltanah's only encounter with a political head of state occurs in Washington, D.C., during his tour of the White House. This visit also appears to be interwoven into Mu'in al-Saltanah's sightseeing and does not come across as premeditated. On the day that he and his interpreter visit the Con-

---

1. I have inserted punctuation into my translations of the Persian text. As I have pointed out, almost no punctuation exists in the Persian text. I am conscious of the inevitable changes my own tampering with Mu'in al-Saltanah's travelogue bring about.

gress, they proceed to the White House, where apparently at that time there were scheduled biweekly audiences with the president for anyone passing through, citizens and visitors alike. Mu'in al-Saltanah remarks that the visitors are asked to congregate in a large audience hall where the president arrives and greets the guests. This is how he describes his own experience:

> We waited with others in this hall. The president entered. His name is Mr. Cleveland. One by one the guests shook his hand. When my turn came, I also shook his hand and told him that I am from Persia and have come to see the Chicago Exposition. I then presented my card to him. He expressed delight in the fact that I had undertaken such a long journey in order to see the United States and wished me an enjoyable visit. In turn, I thanked him. The president left the hall for his own quarters, and the visitors dispersed. (328)

This is the limit of Mu'in al-Saltanah's interest in the political leader of the United States, whom he seems to hold in much less awe than the pope. But there is little overlap between the Persian and the American modes of government. Mu'in al-Saltanah's blasé attitude toward this meeting is echoed in his lack of interest in political events taking place in the United States during his visit.

As a historical document, Mu'in al-Saltanah's travelogue demonstrates certain shortcomings, but as a narrative of personal and cultural identity it proves to be fascinating. As we shall see, Mu'in al-Saltanah's economic and social status filters through his perceptions of alterity, especially the manner in which he often conflates race and class. I should add that my use of the term "identity" does not refer to details of Mu'in al-Saltanah's personal life, about which he is largely reticent. In the preface to the travelogue, he tells his readers that he was a native of Isfahan who had settled in Rasht, near the Caspian Sea, and developed an interest in the cultivation of silkworm. The pursuit of this line of business was very much on his mind during his travels in Europe, as evidenced in his purchase of silk larvae he shipped home. The little we know of Mu'in al-Saltanah's background can be summed up in his status as a merchant eager to learn about new developments in the West. But even this zest for knowledge becomes shrouded in his painstaking record of everything he sees. In Shahidi's view, the abundance of detail in the travelogue forestalls expressions of Mu'in al-Saltanah's views on the peoples and the customs of the lands he visited:

> When he describes all that he has encountered in the course of his journey to Europe and America, he enters into such detail that at times it seems rather tiresome. Yet the detailed descriptions immerse the reader in the proper ambience and setting.
>
> Sometimes he makes a passing reference to the manners and social customs of the inhabitants of the cities he visits. Perhaps his weakness consists of having devoted more attention to the layout of the cities than to their inhabitants. (12)

What Shahidi fails to see is that Mu'in al-Saltanah's meticulous attention to detail is the most crucial component of, if not the driving force behind, his travelogue. It was, in fact, the strange animals, bizarre fruit, new machines, instruments, and mechanical advances of all kind that motivated Mu'in al-Saltanah to keep a record of his travels and to describe what he knew would be novelties for his compatriots.

When he sees a banana for the first time, he provides its name, *banan,* where it normally grows, along with an exact description of its shape and taste: "it looks like an eggplant . . . when ripe, it is yellow. Inside it is like a melon with a sweet and sour taste" (436). On a visit to a zoo, he confesses: "I saw many different animals there which I did not recognize. . . . There are cages holding mice as big as apes, which I am told, are from Mexico. Even more bizarre is that, in another cage, there were apes as small as mice" (301). Sometimes his own attempts at clarifying the novelties become sources of further confusion. For instance, when he sees a buffalo, he confuses the name of the animal with that of a region: "on display are the cattle from the land of Buffalo. . . . The entire body of these cattle is covered with long wool that is dragged on the ground. Their necks are short, and their heads are amazingly large" (358).

Mu'in al-Saltanah was also mesmerized by the infinite possibilities of modern technology he saw in Europe and the United States. The objects, devices, and factories he describes meticulously in his diary did not exist in Persia and had to be demystified and made tangible. Mu'in al-Saltanah's descriptions seem to have a secondary, utilitarian function: as he buys silkworm larvae and transports them back to Persia to set up his own cultivation, he provides methodical enough outlines of other items of novelty so that they might be imitated by Persian artisans. To this end, he spends hours visiting factories and requesting to have their operations explained to him. In this sense, one of his goals is indeed to write an almost graphic catalogue of what he saw in the course of his journey. If the objects he describes are already known to us and are in most cases surpassed by much more complex technical inventions, we must not forget the original allure and promise they had for Mu'in al-Saltanah and his readers. Even the tedium of reading about the layout of bathroom stalls and the functioning of toilet bowls (354), or the description of what, he finds to his amazement, are called "Turkish baths" (294) has to be measured in historically relative terms.

We glimpse the intensity of his own enthusiasm in his train journey to Nice. What becomes the focal point of this trip is his amazement at tunnels. The passage in which he describes the way nature has been adapted to modern transportation has almost a poetic touch:

> After two hours of riding through arid lands, we reached the sea coast. Here the railway has to move northward. Sometimes we pass through wooded areas, other times through green plains, and sometimes through mountains. . . . Slowly the railway approaches the sea. . . . In some spots, the waves come very close to the railway. After some distance, we began to pass through high mountains and we started going through tunnels. Inside these tunnels, there are periodic openings on the side of the mountain facing the sea that provide vistas onto the sea. . . . Near sunset, the rays of the sun are reflected on the

surface of the water. It is so pleasant and makes one enjoy the air. The sea water is visible as if in a painting. When we were passing through one of these tunnels, I counted thirty one-vistas on the sea. I regretted that on the previous occasions I had not done the same thing. (254–55)

The source of Mu'in al-Saltanah's regret is not that he is unable to record the number of tunnels he has passed through on his way to Nice, but rather that his readers will not have a complete vision of the complex constructions which the numbers would have further emphasized. The nature of the inventions he comes across are always at the forefront of his writing. For example, when he sees a guillotine during a play, he feels compelled to give a full description of how it works and to emphasize its efficacy by pointing out the wide and heavy "blade" attached to the contraption that is brought down on to the head and "cuts it like cheese" (265). We cannot necessarily restore Mu'in al-Saltanah's fascination to its origins, but historical accuracy itself would seem to argue against dismissing his descriptions as tedious. In Mu'in al-Saltanah's passion for technology there are the seeds of the drive to modernization that was to sweep Persia a decade later and bring about not merely a technological, but also a cultural revolution.

There are still other historical factors that contribute to the impression that Mu'in al-Saltanah's text consists primarily of a long list of descriptions. I have already alluded to the absence of punctuation in the text, which makes for sentences that run into each other and form long chains with no apparent breaking points. In the most illustrative descriptions, the lack of punctuation produces a breathless reading and leaves the sense that there is little beyond the graphic details. As a result, it is sometimes easy to miss hints of irony, sarcasm, or personal insights woven into the dense fabric of Mu'in al-Saltanah's text.

Mu'in al-Saltanah himself alludes to the condensed nature of his text. In the section of his diary pertaining to his visit to the Vatican, he appears to be overwhelmed by the enormity of the task he has set himself. Well into this description which includes exact measurements of the edifice of the cathedral, he writes: "were I to really describe it, I would have to write many books" (238). In a later segment, he describes his daily entries in these terms: "in reality, each line is a book" (382). Into these comments on Muʻin al-Saltanah's experience of sensory overload is interwoven recognition of the colossal effort required to give a verbal representation of the visual. That seeing, rather than writing, was Muʻin al-Saltanah's primary focus comes across in a passage devoted to paintings he sees at the Chicago Exposition: "I think that these paintings are intended solely for the Americans themselves and not for the tourists. If they are for the travelers passing through, there are so many of them and the faces are so well painted that no matter how long a traveler's stay he will not succeed in completely grasping and appreciating them. They must be intended for the Americans who can be here for the duration of the Exposition and will have the time to fully take them in" (407). Muʻin al-Saltanah's privileging of seeing over communicating verbally has to be understood in light of his dependence on interpreters and his inability to speak European languages, which barred his direct access from anything but the visual. He tried to see as much as possible, but if, as he admits, something gets lost in his translation of the visual into verbal, there is more to his text than meets the eyes. Closer readings of Muʻin al-Saltanah's dense and laborious entries shed light on a larger problem of communication through which he had to negotiate his observations and perceptions.

During most of his trip he was dependent on the services of interpreters who acted as his guides. His relationship to interpreters plays a significant role in determining the very style in which he writes his travelogue. In a sense, Muʻin al-Saltanah's detailed descriptions replicate the same mechanisms of translation through which the linguistic go-betweens helped him decipher the unknown lands and peoples he came across. It is the interpreters he engaged in the course of his trip who provided him with the wealth of information he in turn conveys to his readers. That sometimes he was at their mercy is revealed in some of the inaccuracies he reports without realizing what he was told was meant in jest. For instance, during the visit to the Vatican I have already referred to, he sees a confessional box for the first time. This is how he explains its function: "In this edifice, there is a place where the priests give people absolution. All around the church there are many doors by which cubicles have been placed. These have a side door. The upper half of this door opens both out and to the side. The priest enters this cubicle and shuts the door. Those who have committed sins pass a little money to the priest and confess their sins through an opening in the door. The priest offers them absolution and sells them a piece of heaven" (221). Mu'in al-Saltanah does not attribute this explanation to a guide, nor does he identify him, as, for instance, he does in the case of the interpreter who accompanies him to the States. But there is little doubt that what he saw was affected by explanations he took as authoritative. Similarly, Mu'in al-Saltanah weaves together physical description of the cathedrals and monuments he sees in the Vatican with a brief explanation of the role the clergy play in Italy's political life:

> The pope's residence is large and is beside the same church. It is connected to the church via a door. The pope lives in this place. Given that there cannot be two kings in one country, the kingdom of Italy tries its best to control the pope's interactions with the people. Guards surround this area and survey the paths in and out of the building so that the pope does not get out and join forces with the Catholics to topple the government. The pope is the head of the Catholics and the believers of this faith see him as a special envoy (caliph) descended from Christ. . . . Until recently, popes used to sell parcels of heaven to their disciples, or sometimes just give them away for free. Even now some of their staunch followers try to purchase a spot in heaven, and in those cases a title deed bearing the pope's signature is given to them and their sins are forgiven. (238)

It is possible that Mu'in al-Saltanah is himself responsible for the way in which he equates the office of the pope with that of a Muslim caliph. He might well have assimilated the information provided to him by his interpreter into the religious and political system familiar to him. It is also possible that his interpreter was a Muslim and attempted to find equivalents between the Catholic and the Islamic systems of governance. In either case, at least those segments detailing the financial transactions and the so-called purchase of pieces of heaven must have some link to the interpreter. It is precisely in Mu'in al-Saltanah's deliberate and inadvertent partial understanding of his interpreters that we find the most fascinating examples of his reflections on his adventures in Europe and North America.

We learn much more about Muʻin al-Saltanah and his travels in the segments concerning his interactions with interpreters and the role they played in shaping his impressions of Europe and North America. An examination of Muʻin al-Saltanah's linguistic dependency and his deliberate attempts to present himself as the primary interlocutor with Europeans he encountered help us to better grasp his self-understanding as firmly anchored in the ethos of Persian culture and his assiduous efforts to stave off any threats to the edifice of his personal and cultural beliefs.

The first mention of an interpreter occurs early in the narrative, when Muʻin al-Saltanah and his merchant friend arrive in Venice. Shortly after finding a hotel, Muʻin al-Saltanah and Haji Muhammad Baqir go for a stroll during which "a local man came up to us and told us that he was familiar with foreign languages. He said that we looked as if we had come to visit the city and offered to become our interpreter. Because he appeared to be a reasonable and honest person, I accepted to take him on as our interpreter" (207). This is all we learn about the first interpreter Muʻin al-Saltanah hires during his travels. It is a measure of Muʻin al-Saltanah's total immersion in his own language and culture that he does not even find it necessary to comment on how this "local man" had come to speak Persian, or that the interpreter speaks German, a language understood by Haji Baqir because of his residency in Vienna. Because Muʻin al-Saltanah gives more prominence to his own role in the hiring of the interpreter, we do not know the extent to which Haji Baqir was already acting as his interpreter. Perhaps the vague reference to the interpreter's knowledge of foreign languages is indicative of Haji Baqir's mediation. This hypothesis gains more credibility in a later episode to which we will turn after examining Muʻin al-Saltanah's visit to Naples. What is striking at this stage of the narrative is that interpreters occupy a purely functional role in Muʻin al-Saltanah's imagination.

By the time they arrive in Naples, however, Muʻin al-Saltanah has already begun to provide a little more information about his interpreters. This is also the first occasion on which he articulates his need for an interpreter. After reporting a walk he takes through part of Naples with his traveling companion, he writes: "When we had finished our sightseeing, we returned home, had dinner, and went to bed. God willing, tomorrow I intend to find an interpreter who can make us understand some things" (220–21). It is curious that he should admit to this incomprehension so soon after he has offered his own rather authoritative comparison of Naples with other European cities.

First remarking on the general absence of hygiene in Naples, he goes on to say: "All the buildings, alleys, parks, and gardens are old. Some new buildings are now being built, but because the city has a large population and most of its inhabitants are not refined and such persons are necessarily without taste, it will probably be a thousand years before they can make their city like others in Europe. Certainly not in the near future will this city look like Vienna or Berlin" (220).

Mu'in al-Saltanah's impressions appear to be already formed. We cannot be certain that Haji Baqir, with his prior knowledge of Italy, is not contributing to what is recorded by Mu'in al-Saltanah. Vienna seems to have been the standard against which Mu'in al-Saltanah assessed other European cities. For instance, when in Liverpool, he says: "We passed through wide streets and attractive shopping areas. This city is not much like Manchester. . . . Apparently it has a population of a million. It is not without some resemblance to Vienna . . . but it will never become Vienna" (276). Mu'in al-Saltanah does not explore the reasons for which Liverpool and Naples fall short of what he has established as the model European city, but that these impressions are closely tied to his having his experiences of Vienna filtered through Haji Baqir becomes evident in his need to find a local informant on the occasion of their visit to Naples. He is eager for some answers to the cause of the disparities between Naples and the European cities he has seen up to this point in his travels. His own explanation hints at economic and class differences, but he seeks confirmation of his conjectures from an interpreter. Here the interpreter's linguistic expertise is subordinated to his command of the wider scope of the city's social and cultural makeup. So, Mu'in al-Saltanah sets out the next day to find an interpreter.

Under his entry for the next morning, he writes: "I got up in the morning and, after eating breakfast, along with the Haji went to the Hotel reception. I asked the manager for an interpreter. He immediately found one and presented him to me. His name was Nan National" (221). The interpreter's first name sounds and reads like the word for bread, in Persian, *nan,* suggesting that Muʿin al-Saltanah probably assimilated the Italian name into his own psychosocial phonology. But his reason for inserting the interpreter's name, however Persianized it might be, into the text are very much tied in with Muʿin al-Saltanah's need to give his subsequent experiences in and around Naples authentication. We see in a later episode that the interpreter does indeed provide him with the opportunity to confirm his first impressions of Naples.

During an outing to Pompeii, Muʿin al-Saltanah and his party stop for lunch in a restaurant where they are so warmly and generously received that Muʿin al-Saltanah remarks: "at no time would the members of one's own household show such kindness" (228). His assumptions about this display of hospitality are, however, quickly dispelled: "I was saying to myself that these foreigners are very hospitable. But after lunch, they presented us with a bill that was far in excess of what we normally paid at other restaurants and the reason for all that unprecedented kindness and friendship became clear. Thank goodness, this important matter did not remain a mystery to me" (228).

There is not much surprise in Muʿin al-Saltanah's reaction. Instead, he seems to be almost relieved to be spared the need to drastically revise his image of Italians. In this instance, the interpreter does not play a major role, but in their next outing, to Mount Vesuvius, the same interpreter appears to contribute in large part to the impressions the Persian forms. This section of the narrative reveals a shift from the Persian's reliance on the translator to himself becoming an authoritative voice capable of communicating with the locals, and it is worth examining in detail.

They are off to a bad start when, on the appointed morning, the interpreter arrives in the company of a German individual to whom he seems to have promised the same excursion. The inclusion of the German tourist hints at the possibility that during the Persians' visit to Italy the operative language was German and that Haji Baqir was translating the Italian interpreter's German into Persian for Mu'in al-Saltanah. Interestingly, there is no indication of the multiple levels of linguistic interchange. In fact, as on previous occasions, Mu'in al-Saltanah places himself at the center of the decisions taken during this expedition. Apparently, he is far less reluctant to admit to his dependency on Europeans than on his Persian traveling companion. This is a necessary step toward focusing the narrative on himself.

There is no direct hint of Mu'in al-Saltanah being annoyed at the interpreter's inclusion of another client in what was supposed to have been time devoted to him and Haji Baqir, but he does speak of having had to wait for the interpreter to arrive. As we find out in his description of the later stages of this outing, delays do create complications. At the moment of the departure, however, Mu'in al-Saltanah appears content enough to be able to embark on this long-awaited tour.

The first hour of their climb is accomplished with the help of a horse-drawn rail carriage, later replaced by three horses and a donkey they hire from a local who also joins their party. Obviously it is through the agency of the interpreter that Mu'in al-Saltanah and his group negotiate their means of travel, but already at a very early stage of their expedition the interpreter fades into the background. The process leading up to this event is in many ways reminiscent of the episode in Pompeii.

After two hours of riding along the foothills, the party comes across a mountain hut. As in the previous episode, the manner in which its inhabitants receive the tourists is remarkably warm: "When the occupants saw us, through the interpreter, they expressed much delight at having made our acquaintance. They raised their hat and, shouting in Italian, told the interpreter they had been eagerly waiting to meet us and were pleased to have us in their midst" (228). Because it is lunch time, the travelers inquire about food. They are told that the only food items available in the house are bread, eggs, and cheese. In another instance of not letting go of his own cultural habits, Mu'in al-Saltanah asks whether they know how to make *Khaginih,* a Persian version of scrambled eggs fried in oil. The matter of fact tone in which Mu'in al-Saltanah records his request suggests he is boldly importing his Persian tastes to the Italian landscape. Not put off by the fact that the Italian villagers

have never heard of *Khaginih*, Mu'in al-Saltanah rolls up his sleeves and pre-
pares lunch for those accompanying him and the four villagers who either all
live in the house or drop in to see the tourists. The beautiful setting, Mu'in
al-Saltanah reports, makes for a pleasurable lunch interrupted only by the ex-
orbitant bill presented to the party at the end of lunch. The previous experience in Pompeii seems to have inured Mu'in al-Saltanah to the villagers'
deceptive behavior. In fact, as he reports his settling of the bill to the satisfaction of the villagers, he associates their pretenses of hospitality with what he
had encountered in the restaurant in Pompeii. In other words, he is beginning
to form an image of Italians closely aligned with his impressions of the people
of Naples before he had acquired the services of an interpreter, the pertinent
part of which was: "most of its inhabitants are not refined and such persons are
necessarily without taste" (220). Mu'in al-Saltanah's earlier conjecture that
the dilapidated appearance of Naples corresponds to an uncouthness in its inhabitants is confirmed in the barely disguised expressions of greed on the part
of the villagers he interprets as further indicators of the Italians' general lack of
culture. These views are further entrenched when he begins to suspect the interpreter of being dishonest. Apart from the fact that he includes another of
his clients with the Persians he has agreed to serve, shortly after this lunch
scene, he abandons his charge altogether.

When, after lunch, the party attempts to reembark on their ascent, they
are told that the railway that would normally carry them to the summit is out
of commission and they must make the journey on foot. In spite of the hard-
ships this presents, for they are told the trek might well take up to five hours,
Mu'in al-Saltanah cannot forgo the sight of the crater. In a rare instance of
separating his own actions and utterances from Haji Baqir's, he notes the
latter's reluctance and his own enthusiasm to undertake the long journey on
foot. Needless to say, this distinction once again makes Mu'in al-Saltanah the
central protagonist in the events that follow.

Soon after they set out, they find out they are being followed by "seven
Italians whose appearance indicates they are laborers and manual workers"
(229). Both Mu'in al-Saltanah's Persian traveling companion and the German
tourist presume them to be robbers, but Mu'in al-Saltanah, who again uses

the interpreter as his intermediary, asks why they are being pursued: "The interpreter answered that their presence will become necessary in the course of our expedition and, because they know that their assistance will be required on the way, they follow us" (229). Not only all their protests to the contrary fail to dissuade the seven men, they seem to produce the curious effect of driving away the interpreter and promoting Mu'in al-Saltanah to the role of linguistic intermediary:

> After a few steps, I noticed the interpreter was missing. We looked around for him to no avail. Little did we know that this poor soul is aware of the difficulties of our passage and that he has relieved himself of these hardships and returned to the place where we stopped for lunch. Once again, we told the men following us that Persians are much more adept at walking than Italians, their presence would be unnecessary, and they should leave us. This produced no result, and they did not turn back. We set out again and had walked for about ten minutes when we called the men to come take our hand, for, without a guide, it was very difficult to continue. They took charge of all three of us and helped us along a few steps before we were so overcome with exhaustion we had to sit down. (230)

Even though the Persians fail to prove themselves gifted climbers, Mu'in al-Saltanah cannot resist inserting his proud, albeit inaccurate, declarations of Persian agility. The assumptions he has already made about the inferior and deceitful Italians appear sufficient justification for his own arrogant generalizations about Persians.

If Mu'in al-Saltanah was indeed the primary interlocutor in this scene, it is unclear how he communicated to the seven self-appointed tour guides. What is interesting is the way Mu'in al-Saltanah reanimates the scene as if the exchanges and the negotiations were carried out with no difficulty in the absence of their linguistic mediator and that he himself readily stepped into the position vacated by the interpreter.

After the two Persians and the German tourist have rested, the ringleader of the seven somehow communicates to the three of them that, given that they will not reach the summit without their assistance, they will agree to guide them there for forty francs. Haji Baqir, who finds the price too high, decides to call their bluff by saying that, if they have to give up on their ascent, they will climb down on their own. But after taking a few steps down and finding this as difficult as the climb up, they reopen negotiations and settle on fifteen francs for the guides' wages. They attach an additional condition that each of the tourists is to be helped up the slope with the aid of a rope held at the top by two of the men, while a third keeps watch from behind. Even this provision is not enough, and Mu'in al-Saltanah reports that, before long, his two companions had to be carried on the porters' backs. He himself would have consented to this method of transportation, had he not feared that the additional weight would have made it more likely for the porter to lose his footing and cause both of them to tumble down the mountainside.

This episode takes up a large section of the descriptions, partly owing to its adventurous nature. But I would argue that, aside from its dramatic potential, this excursion also represents one of the rare moments when Mu'in al-Saltanah is cut adrift from an interpreter. The painstaking detail in which he depicts the various stages of their journey and its unexpected twists and turns also reveals his pride in having managed to survive without the help of a local intermediary. This is probably why he does not make any mention of Haji Baqir's knowledge of German and his earlier role in communications between Mu'in al-Saltanah and others. For this episode to become an example of an adventure whose success can be attributed to Mu'in al-Saltanah, Haji Baqir cannot be given a voice and a part earlier in Naples and Pompeii.

Mu'in al-Saltanah's achievements without any knowledge of Italian are remarkable feats he underlines repeatedly by presenting the many negotiations he had to conduct with their Italian guides. He is careful not to dwell unduly on communication problems they would have encountered, nor to bring any attention to the possibility of Haji Baqir's involvement in these exchanges. But one of his attempts to give himself a more direct and prominent role in the dealings with the seven guides goes too far. He slips in a comment about the regional accent of one of the porters which, given his lack of familiarity with Italian, suggests the presence of an intermediary in this particular exchange: "One of the people who was keeping an eye on my movements from behind paused for a rest. I proceeded a couple of steps on my own before having no choice but to call him to my aid. In the language of Italian peasants, he asked: 'if I take you by the hand, will you give me some money for cigarettes?' I accepted graciously under the condition that he get me safely to my destination" (231–32). Understandably Mu'in al-Saltanah does not wish to downplay what was probably a significant role in bargaining with the self-proclaimed tour guides. In fact, what Mu'in al-Saltanah lacked in linguistic proficiency he made up for in his expertise in the art of bartering. His repeated pledges to reward the porters with cigarette money after they had reached their destination pay off. Not only are they escorted to the crater, they are also guided back to the mountain hut where their interpreter has been awaiting their return.

By the time we have reached this stage of the narrative, Mu'in al-Saltanah does not need to mention that the interpreter has proven himself redundant. But this redundancy is specific to the situation at hand. In London and Paris, there are official representatives from the Persian government, merchants, and students on whose services and goodwill he can draw. But when he cannot call upon Persians living in Europe and as soon as Haji Baqir leaves his company, his dependency on interpreters takes center stage once again. For his voyage to the United States, in fact, Mu'in al-Saltanah has to take more serious measures and hire an interpreter who will accompany him every step of the way. As Mu'in al-Saltanah's sole means of access to the New World, this individual acquires a particular position of privilege, albeit modulated by class distinctions, in the Persian's imagination.

Through a Persian studying in London he finds "a man by the name of Murad . . . who resides in Manchester . . . Murad knows Persian, Arabic, Turkish, French, English, and Italian well and is a proficient interpreter in all six languages" (269–70). Murad's own heritage is not remarkably clear. His name, if in fact it is accurately transliterated by Mu'in al-Saltanah, could be Persian or Indian, but when on their way to New York they stop in Manchester and stay with Murad's family, his father's name turns out to be Mr. Shamton. If we do not learn more about Murad, nevertheless, we witness the development of bond between Mu'in al-Saltanah and Murad that carefully preserves the boundaries of class and origins. On the occasion of boarding the ship for their voyage to New York, Mu'in al-Saltanah is separated from Murad because the translator is a second-class passenger:

> We boarded the launch and moved toward the ship. In this launch there were a few first-class passengers. It took us approximately an hour to reach the ship. Because I had a first-class ticket, I went to that part of the ship. Mr. Murad, along with all the others who were second-class passengers had gotten off their launch, boarded the ship, but were kept in a section and were not allowed to move. I stood in a corner and watched them in order to find out the reason for their being detained. A rope was brought and pulled in front of the group. A doctor arrived and stood in front of the rope and examined every one of the passengers. He took about a second to examine each person. He gave some a shake, or opened their mouths and then sent them away. He examined Mr. Murad in this manner and allowed him to enter the ship. . . . As I found out later, the holders of a first-class ticket are not inspected by the ship's doctor. (277)

Although Mu'in al-Saltanah does not question his own right to first-class accommodation, he is puzzled by a form of marking class he has not seen before. His curiosity is provoked by the emptiness of the rushed medical examination. He seems to take note of the fact that the process is an exercise in policing and reinforcing the separation of social classes. If in this episode Murad is part of the object lesson, in other instances he is granted a temporary reprieve from his own status to become integrated in Mu'in al-Saltanah's own policing enterprise.

Mu'in al-Saltanah's visit to San Francisco's Chinatown becomes the focus of one such effort. The trip to San Francisco was conceived of as an extension of the Exposition and many visitors, like Mu'in al-Saltanah and his interpreter, continued on to San Francisco from Chicago. For Mu'in al-Saltanah, this tour constitutes a first encounter with the Chinese. Although he has seen the China exhibit in Chicago, those visits have not given him the sense of immediacy and proximity he experiences in San Francisco's Chinatown.

On this occasion, Mu'in al-Saltanah and Murad hire a local informant recommended to them by a tour guide: "If you decide to have a comprehensive tour of this people, their neighborhoods, and sites, it would be best for you to be accompanied by our chief's son, who has connections with these people" (449). This insider is later, somewhat unexpectedly, described as the police chief's son. This might explain his low opinion of the Chinese. Mu'in al-Saltanah's implicit trust in anything he is told by his guide, in turn relayed by the interpreter, becomes evident in a visit to a teahouse. Mu'in al-Saltanah, Murad, and the guide arrive at the cafe, sit down, and order tea:

> Given their past familiarity, when the Chinese waiter saw the chief of police's son, he became very happy and animated. He left us to go and make tea. With much delight and joy, he brought a copious setting that he placed on the table. There was a China bowl in which he poured the tea and warm water. He then placed a saucer over the bowl for the tea to steep. There were also a few cups with missing handles apparently meant to be used as tea cups. . . . This waiter moved back and forth so fast that he made me and the interpreter, Mr. Murad, laugh. (450–51)

Mu'in al-Saltanah's insistence on observing the bizarre tea cups is here coupled with Murad's participation in investing the scene with other indications of oddity. In his description of the tea cups, Mu'in al-Saltanah could use the word bowl, but he insists on calling the vessel a cup and then pointing to its inadequacy: the missing handle. From this shortcoming, we move to the hectic, "unnatural," movements of the Chinese waiter. It is as much the pace of his movements as what the observers assume to be his physiological differences that bring about the mirth. Mu'in al-Saltanah and Murad form a fraternity that reinforces their own sense of being different from the Chinese they have come to observe.

A similar tone of incredulity and distance permeates a dining scene they witness in Chinatown: "A group of Chinese showed up for lunch. All silent, they stared at each other with immense bewilderment. In front of some of them there was a rice vat filled with water. Each has a bowl in front of him and, holding two bamboo shoots in his hands, picks up the rice grain by grain and eats it" (451). Having never seen chopsticks before, Mu'in al-Saltanah does not have a term by which to refer to them. There is no Persian equivalent he can evoke, and the translation he offers, *qalam,* has a closer association with a writing implement than an eating utensil. A *qalam* in today's Persian means a pen. I have translated it as "bamboo shoot," taking into account that at the time it would have probably referred to a writing instrument made out of bamboo shoots. The first striking aspect of this passage is the incongruity of eating with a writing implement. Given that the use of cutlery was not yet widespread in Persia, it is particularly ironic that Mu'in al-Saltanah should find the Chinese method of eating so difficult to countenance.

As if the bizarre cutlery were not sufficient indicators of the primitive existence of the Chinese workers congregated in this ramshackle café for lunch, Mu'in al-Saltanah draws attention to their facial expressions and links them to the Chinese dependence on opium: "These people's faces have turned black from excessive smoking of opium. Their bodies are weak and emaciated. I was told that they are each paid four dollars a day by the government. Because of their poverty, the government agents ensure that they receive their wages every day, which they spend on opium and the wasting away of their bodies. They have no other pastime" (451). This peculiar blending of pity and blame and the reference to pastime betray Mu'in al-Saltanah's equation of race and class.

These scenes are reminiscent of some of Mu'in al-Saltanah's encounters in Italy, specifically the account of his successful negotiations during the Vesuvius expedition. The superior attitude he adopts vis-à-vis the uncouth villagers is translated here into complicity with his interpreter, on whom he relies during the American journey to fortify his own sense of self.

There is a graphic representation of the dependency, reliance, and support developed between Mu'in al-Saltanah and Murad in the only daguerreotype included in the volume that is not of monuments and sites, but of the two men.

In the background we see the Niagara Falls. Seated on rocks is Mu'in al-Saltanah and standing behind him, slightly off to the side as if not to over-shadow the Falls, is Murad. While Murad holds onto to his cane, Mu'in al-Saltanah has his resting against the rocks. Their poses are also quite differ-ent from one another. Murad looks directly into the camera, while Mu'in al-Saltanah looks off to the side, as if preoccupied with maintaining his bal-ance and the regal pose he has struck by placing both hands on his lap and sit-ting with an uncomfortably straight back. It is hard to miss his hat, which is Persian-style, as are Murad's watch chain and tie. What creates the overall im-pression of Mu'in al-Saltanah's precarious position is the way in which he needs to maintain his pose by lifting one foot and resting it as an anchor against a rock slightly closer to the ones on which he is seated. Murad's posi-tion between Mu'in al-Saltanah and the Falls gains symbolic import. Murad's role was also to buffer Mu'in al-Saltanah from the torrent of information the Persian was eager to witness from a safe distance. The image of Mu'in al-Saltanah straining to maintain his pose is an apt graphic reminder of his continuous struggle to fortify his personal and cultural poise against the on-slaught of curiosities. If he willingly drifted in a sea of technological novelty, he was reluctant to lose his moorings in differences of race and culture.

During his visit to the Chinese exhibit in Chicago, Mu'in al-Saltanah comes across a painting he describes and interprets: "an old Chinese man rid-ing a cow . . . he is wearing fine clothes. From his clothes, one can ascertain that he is a notable among the Chinese and that even the Chinese notables ride cows. The eyes of the cow depicted in the picture are very narrow. It would appear that the animals of this country have the same slanted eyes as its people. In another painting, they have drawn a horse and this horse's eyes are also narrow" (407). This passage is an interesting example of Mu'in al-Saltanah's earlier admission that each of his sentences could tell volumes. His gaze discerns a catalogue of differences that relegate the Chinese to the edges of the human race. The resemblances he finds between the eyes of hu-mans and animals complement the strange practice of riding cattle instead of horses.

American Indians, like Chinese, fall under this category of the alien. His visit to the Native American section of the Exposition follows immediately after the first visit to the section pertaining to China. He finds the Native American mode of dress and their habitat most peculiar. In an example of shared confusion with his interpreter, he translates the term for American Indian as *Hindi-yi Amrika'i* literally the East Indians of the United States. As if to eradicate an inappropriate conflation of these Indians with the inhabitants of the Indian subcontinent, he immediately adds: "the savages of America whose skin is completely red" (361). The description that follows further qualifies his understanding of the term savage: "I bought a ticket and entered the area. The display takes up a vast space around whose periphery simple tents are erected. In the middle, there is a modest white tent inside which there is a platform. On the platform there is a drum and around it seven people, each bearing a stick, are sitting and hitting the drum. Two of them also cry out [*faryad mikunand*]. In reality, this crying is their song" (362). The word *faryad* has many connotations in Persian, some steeped in a poetic sense of giving voice to or crying out. Without eliminating these possible connotations, I would like to emphasize that in Mu'in al-Saltanah's usage *faryad* is clearly distinguished from *avaz* (song). The rest of this description does little to make up for Mu'in al-Saltanah's earlier defamiliarizing representations of Native Americans. When he runs out of terms to describe the native dress, for instance, he points out that what covers the lower half of the body is made of strips that look like fly swatters. This rounds off his depictions of Native Americans' primitiveness and brings them closer to the Chinese.

If in Mu'in al-Saltanah's imagination there is one strand linking the Native Americans, the residents of San Francisco's Chinatown, and the other Americans of European origin, it is precisely the hint of savagery he notes even in the most modernized and well-equipped American city he visits. During his stay in Philadelphia, for instance, he takes immense delight in the natural beauty and charms of a public garden where a band performs a concert. But his enjoyment is undercut by a most unlikely reminder:

> I drank a cup of tea and began exploring this area. This part of the garden is more elevated and opens onto the rest of the garden. But we will not go any

farther than the band players. That is to say, I dare not take ten steps beyond this point. The citizens here are not the most honest and upright people. With the exception of a small minority, the rest are savages. If someone wanders into a dark corner of the park, he risks his life. . . . It is clear from the appearance of this garden that it is new and that the people of this town would like to imitate the Europeans. It is evident that they are not by nature civilized. (299)

Mu'in al-Saltanah's impressions of the lack of civility in American cities go beyond these first impressions in a public garden in Philadelphia. In a later episode, he remarks:

> The explorers who have seen Europe and Philadelphia can attest that these people's manners and appearances are different from those of Europeans. There are many rough and tumble, and ruffians from all over the world gathered here. Among them are many thieves. For example, one evening, not three hours past sunset, I entered my hotel. When I began climbing the stairs to my own room, I saw a man holding a stick standing in the doorway. I thought he was a thief. I stopped and he approached me and said: "your room at such and such a place is open, please proceed and shut your door afterwards." It turns out that this person is an employee of the hotel and his task is to guard the hotel rooms all night long. Never mind that this is one of Philadelphia's most reputable hotels. If there is such absence of safety here, you can imagine what it is like for the citizens of Philadelphia and the people of the United States. (317–18)

This image of America as the hinterland of civilization is epitomized in Mu'in al-Saltanah's declarations that "even the savages of this country are more savage than the savages of Europe" (295). As Mohammad Ghanoonparvar has noted, Mu'in al-Saltanah reserves an ambivalent attitude toward American society (1993, 30). But these ambivalences are deeply rooted in discursive notions of the self and the other that are continuously renegotiated to arrive at a resounding affirmation of the Persian frame of reference.

When Mu'in al-Saltanah perceives an attack on the honor and reputation of Persians, he musters a rhetoric of communal identification in which we can discern the parameters distinguishing the self from the other. Even in his most trenchant critiques of life in parts of Europe and the United States, Mu'in al-Saltanah never draws comparisons with Persia. His own country is never depicted and discussed; it remains Mu'in al-Saltanah's unassailable inner compass.

It is his visit to the Persian exhibit that provokes his ire. He discovers that the Persian display is masterminded by a "Jewish person" who has acquired the concession right from the Persian government and in whose pay are Persians who, like Mu'in al-Saltanah, find aspects of the exhibit objectionable:

> In the upper hall of this building, this Jewish person has dressed a few French women in Persian costume and has falsely presented them as Persian women. These women dance for the entertainment of the public. . . . As male honor [*ghayratmandi*] is a crucial characteristic of a Muslim, the Persians working for the Jew became angry and offended at the Jew's barbaric act of dressing French women in Persian clothes, mis-presenting them as Persian women, and making them dance. They have banded together and threatened to close down their displays. The news has reached the Jew, who, for fear of losing his operations, changed the women's dress back to Parisian outfits. But the Persians are still determined to expel the women from the exhibit so that in a place designated as Persian such matters of ill-repute do not occur. (369)

This is where Mu'in al-Saltanah abruptly leaves off his account of the Persian exhibit. We do not find out if the designation "French women" is a euphemism for the women's profession. The official record of the Exposition, the *Book of the Fair,* gives some credence to this hypothesis: "Adjoining this exhibition is the Persian palace, which reproduces a portion of the royal residence of the shah of Ispahan, the large hall on the first floor being decorated with all the richness of coloring characteristic of Persian taste. On the second floor are a restaurant and a tea house. . . . Although the café contains, besides its black-eyed waiters, a number of dancing girls, there is a special hall in another part of the palace, in which are entertainments of a questionable character" (863).

In the *Book of the Fair*, there is photograph of a woman with the caption, "Persian Dancing Girl" (585). These two mutually exclusive sources intersect in their independent evocations of the female body for the construction of a communal, if not, national identity. The Orientalist assumptions of the *Book of the Fair* recall an archive of images of Persian harems and dancing girls, while Mu'in al-Saltanah's invokes *ghayratmandi* to counter this challenge to the Persian sense of pride. Grafted onto Mu'in al-Saltanah's notion of Persianness is a necessary affiliation to the Shi'ite community of believers, set sharply against his assumption of the statelessness of the Jewish person. In Benedict Anderson's words, this racism "does not simply express an ordinary political enmity. It erases nation-ness" (1983, 148). Extending Anderson's argument to Mu'in al-Saltanah's representations of racial difference, be it Chinese, Native American, or Jewish, we might find reasons for the frequent conflation of race and class in his travel narrative: "The dreams of racism actually have their origins in ideologies of *class*, rather than in those of nation; above all in claims to divinity among rulers and to 'blue' or 'white' blood and 'breeding' among aristocracies" (Anderson 1983, 149). Mu'in al-Saltanah's language does not allude to an aristocracy of blood, but he does indeed subscribe to a belief in the inherent valuation of class and its inexorable convergence with Persian cultural identity.

Mu'in al-Saltanah's own identity, formidably deeply entrenched in ideas of class and culture, is rarely shaken. As we have seen in his representation of his role in the Vesuvius expedition, he eliminates barriers of language and culture in order to regain control and superiority. There are, however, a few instances in which this process of self-affirmation is encumbered by the presence of languages and cultural practices he does not grasp. On such occasions, we see a far less self-possessed tourist conscious of being suddenly cut off from all that is familiar and comforting.

In one of his first evenings aboard the ship traveling to New York, he is jolted out of his sleep by a foghorn: "Such a sound was issued from the ship's horn that I was awakened. The sounds were dreadful and I was truly terrified" (281). If "truly terrified" does not convey the extent to which he is traumatized by the sound of the foghorn, the entry following this sentence makes it amply evident. The anxiety Mu'in al-Saltanah experiences that night is immediately juxtaposed with a friendly encounter he has with one of the passengers the next day at lunch. The absence of punctuation makes for a most intriguing sequence of events with no interruption between his report of being startled by the foghorn and the scene of camaraderie the following day:

> At the lunch table, I made a friend. That is to say, I began talking to a person sitting beside me and we formed a friendship. Yet, as long as we talked, neither of us asked the other's name. There is a book in which the passengers register their names. He pointed to my name and asked me if that was it. I said yes. Then he showed me his own name. The next day I sat in a different part of the dining hall. That day I met two other individuals seated next to me. We became friendly and chatted. It was very enjoyable. None of us inquired about the other's name.

Most striking is the combination of Mu'in al-Saltanah's apprehension, mingled with a sense of being out of his element, and the sudden familiarity he discovers among total strangers. He is quick to point out he made a friend, even if that friendship provides him only with a passing illusion of companionship. That even these brief encounters leave him alienated and lonely is underlined in his remark that he never got to know these strangers by name. The pretense of friendship helps him overcome his fear of potential danger during the crossing, but it is not long before he finds himself irrevocably cut off from the company of the other passengers.

It is interesting that the liminal space encapsulated by being aboard a ship produces yet another experience of alienation in Mu'in al-Saltanah. During one of the evenings a concert is organized for the entertainment of the ship's passengers. When Mu'in al-Saltanah realizes that tickets are being sold for this event, he buys one and attends it. To his surprise, the storminess of the sea does not interrupt the event. Aside from his fellow passengers' disregard for their safety, he finds other sources of incomprehension:

> At eight o'clock, piano music and singing could be heard from the library. Everyone gathered there, including myself. More than a hundred first-class passengers were seated and were either looking about or engaged in conversation. I sat down, dazed that none of these people was giving a thought to being in the middle of sea being rocked about by waves. Should we not at least say a prayer and ask God to ensure a safe passage for us? All of them are watching the women who are singing and playing the piano. . . . After this, everyone in the room began singing. I too cried out [*faryad mikardam*] with them lest they think me a stranger and a foreigner. Still, they could tell from my voice and facial expression that I was a stranger. (282)

Mu'in al-Saltanah's desire to conform with what he assumes to be customary practice is touchingly at odds with his own sense of being out of place. His singing along while knowing that it does not sound and look right to others is in sharp contrast with some of his bravado, especially in Italy, where he finds most people lacking in culture. But being aboard a vessel constantly reminding him of his own precariousness, he is painfully conscious of his borderline existence. It is most befitting that he should decide to put on his own little performance inside the other staged event. Even more apt is his reference to his own singing in terms he later uses to describe Native American singing. His awareness of his status as an outsider places him in a rank not unlike those he cannot easily fit into the American landscape. In this difficult moment of crossing, Mu'in al-Saltanah is at least temporarily transformed into one of those "savages" whose singing resembles senseless crying.

What such episodes point up is that, while Mu'in al-Saltanah is engaged in recording all the novelties and anomalies he comes across, he often feels himself an outsider. This second current running through his diary, the consciousness of being the true alien in the lands he visits, is much more subtle, but can nevertheless be teased out of a few incidents recorded by Mu'in al-Saltanah.

In Chicago, he is reminded that his appearance is exotic. During a walk in a park, he and his interpreter pause for a rest and the following scene unfolds:

An older man and woman were holding a newspaper and reading it. Periodically, they would throw a furtive glance in my direction. I went closer to them, and they too approached me and we greeted each other. They asked me where I was from. I asked about the purpose of their inquiry. They pointed out that, in the newspaper they were reading, it was reported that a Persian had been visiting accompanied by a interpreter. They said that they had guessed from my clothes that I must be that person and the other individual to be my interpreter. I confirmed that I was the said Persian and that the fellow with me was my interpreter and that we had come as visitors. They were very pleased with their own guess. (437)

Apart from the older man and woman's recognition of him from his clothes, Mu'in al-Saltanah is also made aware of the fact that he is enough of an object of curiosity to be written about in the daily paper. The excitement and the wonder of the Exposition seem to have in no way detracted from attention to Mu'in al-Saltanah's presence. Unbeknownst to the Persian, he himself has become a traveling exhibit. Although he is gracious in engaging the couple in a conversation and satisfying their curiosity, his asking about the purpose of their query betrays his having been taken aback.

Another episode marking fascination with Mu'in al-Saltanah takes place in Philadelphia, while he is touring the city's parks:

I sat down on a bench. An older man came and sat down beside me and we exchanged a few words. I asked him about the statues. . . . I could tell from his appearance of this man that he was well-to-do. He is originally from Germany and has lived in Philadelphia for forty years. He wrote down his name in my diary. . . . I wanted to also write his name in Persian. He kept looking at my diary and was surprised at Persian writing. He asked me to write a little in my book in his presence so that he could watch. I wrote a little about the garden. He was terribly amazed at the sight of the Persian alphabet. I wrote down my own name for him and gave it to him. He thanked me, we shook hands, and parted company. (309–10)

The German immigrant and Mu'in al-Saltanah mirror each other's fascination with the alien and the transplanted. While in Mu'in al-Saltanah's writing the German finds a reflection of his exotic origins, Mu'in al-Saltanah struggles to understand the German's forty-year displacement. He cannot conceptualize the life of an immigrant. For him, the immigrant remains a German who happens to have lived forty years in Philadelphia. This assumption draws attention to Mu'in al-Saltanah's own concept of cultural belonging. There is no room in his imagination for voluntarily leaving home. To be Persian is to live out one's years in Persia.

Inextricably intertwined with Mu'in al-Saltanah's difficulty in conceptualizing cultural transplantation is his grasp of the crucial link between language and identity. When he is in Liverpool and finds out about British converts to Islam, his curiosity is piqued. Yet he stumbles on a linguistic barrier that prevents him from being able to accept the converts' having crossed over into a realm with which he identifies: "I had heard that a few Englishmen had converted to Islam. They have a noteworthy Muslim congregation in this city. Their spiritual leader is Sheikh 'Abdullah Killam, a very nice man, whose son is named Muhammad and his daughter, 'Ayishih. They have an excellent mosque which they attend on Sundays for prayer services. They have the Qu'ran in English as well as other Persian and Arabic books, but no one can read them" (276–77). The "but" in the last sentence sums up Mu'in al-Saltanah's assessment of the authenticity of these converts' life as Muslims. Because the only Muslims he knows speak either Arabic or Persian, he fails to make the necessary shift in his imagination. Like the German who has immigrated to the United States, for him, they are firmly anchored in origins. The limits Mu'in al-Saltanah imposes on conversion and immigration inevitably circumscribe his own experiences as an early tourist. Dazzled by what he sees, he is nevertheless eager to return. In fact, the last entry in his travelogue indicates the relief with which he has arrived not only in his own country, but also in Rasht, the city he identifies as home. Interestingly, it is not until he has left the Caspian port town of Anzali and traveled the short distance to Rasht that he declares his arrival in "[his] own familiar homeland" (483). To be home again is to shed the heavy armor protecting him from the intriguing, yet foreign, domains he had visited.

This closing sentence raises interesting questions about Mu'in al-Saltanah's notion of home. For all the relief registered in this ending, we have no sense of Mu'in al-Saltanah's life in Persia. This is in part a function of the demands of the kind of narrative he is engaged in writing. This is the age in which many other Persians, particularly those of higher social and political stature, traveled to Europe and wrote extensively about their experiences. Mu'in al-Saltanah's travelogue belongs in this burgeoning genre, avidly read by Persians eager to discover all they could about what were for them exotic nations and customs. As we have seen, Mu'in al-Saltanah himself was completely absorbed by the novelties of Europe and North America. But the curiosities that grabbed his attention were committed to writing for the benefit of others and, even more importantly, for the purpose of cataloguing new advances in science. The power they exert on Mu'in al-Saltanah's imagination is delimited by a sense of cultural self-sufficiency capable of withstanding the encroachment of science. Behind Mu'in al-Saltanah's keen appetite for seeing as much as possible during his journey is an equally intense liking for well-organized and -orchestrated displays with the proper distance between the observer and the observed.

The diary of his travels is such a highly orchestrated endeavor. Far from being a simple documentation, Mu'in al-Saltanah's travelogue is a carefully chiseled narrative of his having passed through a world full of tempting curiosities and having emerged unscathed. His becoming the sole protagonist of the adventures he describes is due to his own manipulations of events, even those that caused him to lose his calm composure and to admit to panic. The writing of the travel diary itself was a means of overcoming those passing moments of anxiety. By transcribing his daily activities in Persian at the end of each day, Mu'in al-Saltanah was able to interpret his experiences as resounding affirmations of his rightful place in his own culture. Being Persian had an even more compelling attraction for him than the wonders he happened to see in the course of his journey.

With increased travel to the West and the accompanying desire to import the fruits of modern science into Persia, Mu'in al-Saltanah's world had already begun to change. Not surprisingly the first modern school, founded in 1851 in Tehran, *Dar al-Funun,* was a polytechnic. The new modes of knowledge brought with them challenges that began to affect the very assumptions that allowed Mu'in al-Saltanah to remain impervious to the inevitable intertwining of knowledge and power. New patterns of thought necessitated self-articulations of a different kind. As we shall see in the next chapter, it would not be long before encounters with the other would instigate new experiments with Persian identity.

3

A New Menu for Alterity

The three-volume work of 'Abdullah Mustawfi, *Sharh-i Zindigani-yi Man* (Description of My Life) offers an interesting instance of life writing interwoven with social history, hinted in the book's subtitle, *A Social and Administrative History of the Qajar Era*. The main and the secondary titles might at first seem to signal two very different projects: the life of an individual as opposed to that of a monarchy. But the two intersect in the Mustawfi lineage.

Beginning with 'Abdullah Mustawfi's great-grandfather, the men of this family became revenue administrators for the Qajar kings who ruled Persia between 1779 and 1925. The family name itself signifies their hereditary office: "The financial business of the country had been in the hands of a small number, only about a score, of officials called Mustaufis, revenue receivers. Their duties and specialised knowledge of the tax regime had tended to pass from father to son" (Avery 1965, 149). 'Abdullah Mustawfi's career, however, developed along a different line: he received training in foreign affairs and political science in Tehran, and in 1904 he was appointed to a diplomatic post in the Persian consulate in St. Petersburg, where he served for five and a half years.

During this period, Mustawfi traveled to other parts of Europe and visited major Western European cities, among them London, Paris, Vienna, and Berlin. His term of office in Europe was followed by many years of service in various government ministries in Persia. Although I will be touching upon aspects of Mustawfi's life and career in Persia, my analysis is more closely focused on his experiences in the West and the ways in which they shaped his sensibil-

ities and bolstered his belief in the need to revamp Persian linguistic and na
tional identity. Mustawfi's posting in Europe coincided with a period of Persian cultural history in which the encounter with the West provided a catalyst
for change. Mustawfi's approach to selective appropriation of European culture is oddly intertwined with his Persian nationalism. For him and many of
his contemporaries, Europe and things European provided useful tools in the
construction of a new national image. More importantly, their mere existence
as counterexamples to Persia and Persians served the important function of
raising questions about matters of tradition, authenticity, and national character. It is precisely the place and function of alterity I wish to explore in
Mustawfi's reflections on life. I should point out that I am not particularly
concerned with the extent to which he was "influenced" or "colonized" by
the West. He is unambiguous in his opposition to economic, political, and
cultural dependency on European nations. What is more central to my analysis is how his being propelled outside the limits of his knowledge and familiarity made Mustawfi internalize alterity and entered him into a contact zone
between the Persian self and the European other. In his work the logic of bi-
naries gives way to a process of transculturation, along the lines delineated by
Mary Louise Pratt in *Imperial Eyes*. The directions she offers for reading the
nature of contacts between imperial centers and their periphery are helpful in
understanding Mustawfi's anxieties about self-representation to Persians as
well as to Europeans: "The fruits of empire, we know, were pervasive in shaping European domestic society, culture, and history. How have Europe's constructions of subordinated others been shaped by those others, by the
constructions of themselves and their habitats that they presented to the Europeans?" (1982, 6).

I will begin with a discussion of the basic structure and mechanics of
Mustawfi's writing in order to arrive at an understanding of the voice that
emerges from the *Description of My Life*. I will then turn to Mustawfi's treatment of language and culture, both Persian and European, and analyze specific scenes that highlight Mustawfi's proclivity for experiments with identity.

We can deduce from the dates of the introduction and conclusion that
Mustawfi seems to have completed his writing over a period of five years: 1942

to 1947. The three volumes did not all appear in print before his death in 1950. Mustawfi's son alerts the readers in a preface appended to the first volume that, at the time of his death, his father had only completed the editing of the first two volumes, but that his handwritten notes in the margins have all been preserved, mostly in the form of footnotes.

Had Mustawfi had enough time to fully revise his text, he might well have altered the first introduction, dated 1942, or at least blended it with the new one he wrote for the third volume. In the introduction to the first volume, he professes a modest goal: *"The Description of My Life* has nothing worthy of reading. My primary aim is a presentation of social history, especially the system and manner of government and administration in the sixty some years of my life. Because the modes of organization and governing, particularly of the pre-Constitutional period, were the product of a different era, I will write about my ancestors in order to better clarify the conditions of my own time. If now and then I write of my own deeds or that of my forefathers, it is solely to elucidate a particular issue pertaining to social or administrative matter, not to aggrandize myself or my ancestors" (1982, 1:1). This is evidently the aim with which Mustawfi embarks on his project. The heading of the first chapter testifies to his careful balancing of family history and the chronicle of the Qajar dynasty: "My Ancestors During the Reign of Aqa Mohammad Khan Qajar." The opening segment is devoted to Mustawfi's great-grandfather and his having gained the trust and confidence of the future monarch, but it is quickly juxtaposed with a description of Aqa Mohammad Khan's own heritage and his characteristics as a fierce and cruel ruler.

Mustawfi maintains this interweaving of the two sets of chronicles, one personal and the other dynastic, even in the chapter dealing with his own birth, although the beginning of a new section is graphically marked in the text bearing the title of the book. The subheading, "Birth," is still somewhat detached, as is the description, which tells us the exact date and place "a boy was born to the owner of the said house and his third wife, lady Zibandih" (152). We are then told the boy was named 'Abdullah, to rhyme with Fathullah, the father's name and that of another son. The large typeface of this section's heading, "Description of My Life," absolves Mustawfi of the need to announce that he is speaking of his own birth. Yet, he seems to have been careful not to reinsert an "I" into the body of the text immediately following the centered heading. This caution reflects the modest tone of the introduction and illustrates the Persian cultural reluctance to emphasize one's individuality.

Mustawfi circumvents the perils of writing about the reigning Pahlavis by limiting himself to the fallen Qajars. Adhering to the historical parameters already delineated in the subtitle of his work, Mustawfi revisits the issue in the closing remarks of the final volume: "Dear reader, what was the title of this book? 'The Description of My Life,' or 'A Social and Administrative History of the Qajar Era.' The Qajar era, good or bad, has come to an end. That is to say, I have lived up to my promise and maintained the premise of the book's title. The remainder of my life history, the intervening twenty some years, does not have much worthy of discussion" (672). The two additional reasons he offers for his decision to wrap up his life history at the end of the Qajar era are: his having spent most of the time he does not write about in the provinces, away from the center of events and, paradoxically, the absence of historical distance from all that has taken place in that period of time. From behind this dual historical and geographical barrier, Mustawfi resists being co-opted into writing a political autobiography celebrating the Pahlavi dynasty.

But Mustawfi is not completely exempt from personal pride; in his writing we see residues of his struggle to contain the self. For instance, he gives us a painstaking account of his paternal household, describing the architecture of the house, the role of the servants, their place in the household, and numerous family rituals. But these details are counterbalanced with broader overviews of social customs of the times. That he leaves room for criticism of placing his own family at the center of life in Qajar Persia is reflected in the defense he has to offer in the preface to the third volume he entitles "Renewed Introduction, Appreciation and Defense." In response to why he devotes so much attention to the architecture of the family house and why he overlooks others' accounts of the Qajar era, Mustawfi writes:

> It is not my fault that my great-grandfather was born in 1768, in other words one hundred and seventy-two years ago, and that he was the first person with

a literary temperament to enter Aqa Mohammad Khan's service. There is no great expanse of time separating me from this great-grandfather. My family's pen was entwined with the Qajar sword. Moreover, if my family and myself were always in government, it is no great event of epic proportions. If I have enough material in my personal and family arsenal on which to base a social and administrative history, what need is there to turn to others? Besides, although my aim in writing has been to elucidate a segment of Qajar history, I should not forget the title of my book, *Description of My Life*, and draw upon other family histories to present the events of the times. (2)

This second introduction realigns his personal life experiences far less ambiguously than the one accompanying the first volume. Mustawfi's defense of the new emphasis on his family and himself stems from his own role in this segment of his historical narrative. Unlike the first volume, which opens with events long before his own birth, the second and the third volumes have given him occasion to come to terms with the importance of his own experiences for the narrative. Precisely when there is an abundance of events to relate from his own life in Europe he repeatedly and boldly reminds his readers that his task should not be confused with that of a historian.

His most interesting disclaimers appear in the second volume and coincide with his treatment of the initial events surrounding the Constitutional Revolution (1905), which he did not witness firsthand. Toward the beginning of volume 2, he points out that his knowledge of events in Persia is based primarily on what his brother communicated to him in letters he received while residing in St. Petersburg. Because of his inability to write from the position of a participant or eyewitness, Mustawfi advises his readers to consult other historical sources. In this same context, responding to potential criticism, he addresses his own reluctance to carry out more extensive research: "As to why I do not consult informants and books to be able to write a comprehensive account, I have no pretensions to writing a history. A description of my life is one thing, the writing of history something altogether different" (163). This defensive posture has once again extracted from Mustawfi an admission that his personal perspective mitigates his use of the term "history" in the title.

As it turns out, Mustawfi's own life has suddenly taken an eventful turn. He is in Europe for the first time and he is overwhelmed by the novelty of all that surrounds him. True to his purpose, however, he does not abandon his pursuit of the description of a parallel process of change taking place in Persia. In fact, this section of the narrative consists of alternating reports from Tehran and records of life in St. Petersburg.

What Mustawfi offers his readers is a nuanced reading of social history. His very insistence on the blending of personal and social history implies his appreciation of the extent to which individuals are the product of the particular family, social, and historical circumstances. The only history he knows is one he has lived himself, or has been told through the annals of the family. He makes no effort to remind his readers of the exact dates of the events he describes, although, throughout the text, he provides broad outlines of historical markers. In other words, while the narrative follows a chronological order, it does not submit to an exact and complete sequence. He gives himself license to select from among the series of events that make up the history of the era in which his project is situated.

Mustawfi's nonchalant attitude toward the exacting requirements of writing history must also be understood in light of his suspicion of the faultiness of memory, individual or collective. In the introduction to the first volume, he declares: "The writing of one's life history is a difficult task, for loss of memory, mistakes, and inherent human weakness can lead us away from the truth" (1). This recognition of the subjective nature of memory may not always be at the forefront of his writing, especially in those moments he takes family lore for irrefutable truth. But, as in his struggle to preserve equilibrium between the personal and the collective, Mustawfi at least signals the issues that are unresolved for him, or remain caught between different traditions and conventions. His approach to the writing of a life history is itself such an example in that it straddles different conventions of autobiographical and historical writing.

At least on one level, his text is couched in didactic terms of *tazkarih*, the traditional biographies of great men. Yet, we see a tension between the purported didactic aim and the stories that emerge from between the cracks in the façade. Mustawfi's life writing offers particularly intriguing instances of sub-texts competing to emerge from the margins.

The narrative is repeatedly interrupted by footnotes, which, on one level, seem to provide supplementary explanations. But their scholarly focus is off-set by highly personal reflections in which we gain glimpses of Mustawfi's character. If Persian literary form discourages him from embarking on a confessional presentation of his life, a scholarly convention he has become acquainted with in the West provides him with the opportunity to experiment with forms of life writing in Persian.

Mustawfi does not necessarily use footnotes for purposes of documenting sources. In fact, most of his footnotes address issues of language and writing, which are at the very core of his preoccupation with the reshaping of identity. In his obsession with language we can detect larger patterns of his visions and ambitions.

Mustawfi's interest in writing and in his mother tongue is evident throughout the three volumes. He has a remarkable habit of explaining Persian idiomatic expressions and sayings in footnotes. Quite often he traces the origin of a given expression and speculates about the habits of mind and customs that gave rise to it. The explanations he offers his readers are not always limited to archaic usage or less current expressions. Sometimes he explains expressions so common that they do not require any elucidation. For instance, in a footnote in volume 1, he points out: " '*dam bih khumrih zadan*' (literally, to put lips to the jug) is an allusion to drinking and drunkenness" (35), or " '*bidi nist kih az in badha bilarzad*'(112), he explains, refers to a person's mettle. He takes sheer delight in taking apart expressions, analyzing their logic, and putting them back together for native speakers who may have never stopped to examine them. But Mustawfi's linguistic vigilance does not stop here. When anecdotes take him away from Tehran, into the provinces, or involve characters who speak different dialects of Persian, he pauses to translate unfamiliar expressions. In one footnote, he provides an extensive pronunciation guide to Isfahani dialect for a couplet whose rhyme can only be appreciated if pronounced correctly.

There are also explanations and translations of numerous Turkish words and phrases. Given the Turkic origins of the Qajar family, the period of Persian history to which Mustawfi is devoting his attention provides him with ample opportunity to comment on the origin of administrative terms that apparently entered Persian via Turkish. Sometimes this type of commentary bears witness to Mustawfi's taking part in a linguistic nationalism that became part of a programmatic plan to "purify" Persian of Turkish and Arabic contamination.[1] For instance, writing about a Qajar office bearing the Turkish title of *ishiyak khanih*, gives him occasion to anticipate with relish its replacement with an "original" Persian term: "Most Persian expressions pertaining to the court are Turkish. The term *bashi*, meaning chief, was current among all the heads of royal offices. But among them, *ishiyak aqasi bashi* had retained its heavy Turkish flavor. As we shall see, this title will soon change to minister of court protocol, and the former *ishiyak aqasis* will be referred to as chief protocol officers" (1982, 1:409). He reports proudly that the Persian equivalent, *salarbar*, existed in pre-Islamic Persian monarchic history and was transmitted into Arabic through Persian and, in turn, later adopted by Turks. For the genealogy of the Persian term, Mustawfi turns to Firdawsi's Persian epic, the *Shah Namih* (Book of the Kings), which has long been celebrated as one of the first expressions of Persian linguistic and national autonomy in the wake of the Islamic conquest of Persia. In the words of Reuben Levy, "The theme that runs throughout the whole poem is . . . the rise and career of the Iranian people" (1969, 67). Persian nationalists of Mustawfi's time as well as later generations found the *Shah Namih* a rich frame of reference for matters of language, national myths, and legends.

Mustawfi's overview of the linguistic transmutations this royal designation has undergone allows him to evoke a pre-Qajar Persia, free of Turkic domination, encapsulated in Firdawsi's Persian epic. In other words, his linguistic commentary gives him a space within which to arrive at an alternative history and a new Persian genealogy. In pursuit of his interests in the origin of words and phrases, Mustawfi begins to compose a counterhistory in which the

---

1. 'Isa Sadiq's *Yadgar-i Omr*, particularly volume 2, provides some interesting insights into this process of linguistic reform.

Qajar Turks can be seen as inheritors of a long tradition of Persian royal customs. What begins as a clarification of official titles brings us closer to understanding Mustawfi's attitude toward Turks and Turkish.

There is evidence of Mustawfi's aversion to Turks in other parts of his life history. In the earliest portions of the first volume, Mustawfi attributes popular resistance to a minister, Haji Mirza Aqasi, to his penurious Turkish habits and his unabashed preferential treatment of Turks at the expense of Persians and other ethnic groups. Citing the Turkish words *bizimki* and *uzgih* (us and them) which he translates into Persian in a footnote, Mustawfi writes: "This was not [the minister's] fault. All Turks behave this way. Someone used to say: if a Turk decides, after a year of deliberation, to give alms to the poor, he will keep the money in his pocket for ten days until he finds a Turkish beggar. Even in giving alms a Turk will want to please his own kind" (49). Paradoxically, Mustawfi's abhorrence of Turkish ethnocentrism makes him intolerant toward the language, which he cannot divorce from the disposition of the ruling class. There is no realization on his part that his own ethnocentrism mirrors the very attitudes he is criticizing among Turks.

Even long after Mustawfi has stepped outside the borders of his own country and come into contact with a number of other languages and cultures, he is unable to shake off his dislike for the very sound of Turkish. For instance, his glowing reports of a first visit to Paris are marred by an episode relating the intrusion of Turkish into his otherwise enjoyable stay. While narrating the manner in which he has acquired a new, most pleasant companion, Luqman al-Dulah, he writes:

Only one thing bothered me: his speaking Turkish with Mr. Safa' al-Mamalik. At last I told them: "Will the two of you, one from Na'in the other from Ashtian, not give up speaking this Mongol dialect imposed by the sword on the natives of Azerbaijan, even in Paris? At least Mr. Luqman al-Dulah was born in Tabriz and spent his childhood there. His speaking Turkish has some foundation, but you, Mr. Safa' al-Mamalik, what justification do you have? Why do you venerate this language of savages?" It was with the aid of this logic that I rid myself of the discomfort of having to listen to this harsh and unpleasant accent that was regrettably imposed on some Persians. (1982, 2:221)

Mustawfi's antipathy toward Turkish is so profound that in his diatribe against the language he inadvertently downgrades it to a dialect. This is one of the most startling expressions of Mustawfi's prejudice against Turks and indirectly touches upon his motivations for blending the history of the Qajar dynasty with that of his own family. Given the central administrative role played by the Mustawfis, he can, in fact, subordinate the Qajar fortune to his own clan's expertise and superior culture. In this manner, the Qajar Turks, though the nominal rulers, are seen as dependent upon Persian talent and know-how.

Mustawfi's intolerant attitude toward Turkish and his assertion of its contamination of Persian are diametrically opposed to his acceptance of interferences from other languages. His linguistic nationalism is not as unbending vis-à-vis Arabic as that of many of his contemporaries who embarked on the systematic eradication of Arabic influences from Persian. That Arabic language and Islamic heritage are part of the Persian cultural tapestry Mustawfi takes for granted. Qu'ranic allusions and direct citations are everywhere visible in his text. He shows a similar open-mindedness with regard to borrowings from European languages, particularly French.

In the discussion of Nasir al-Din Shah's first visit to Europe, he uses the term *asasih-i qudrat*, which, as he explains in a footnote, is a translation of the French *appareil du pouvoir* (machinery of power). He defends its conciseness and usefulness first in characteristic understatement: "in my opinion, it is not a bad expression" (1982, 1:126). Then he gives voice to a notion of linguistic crossbreeding he takes up on several other occasions:

Some writers criticize the use of translation and imitation of foreign expressions and believe it to be against the principles of good writing. In reality, they wish to say that we must not abandon the antiquated *shah tahmasbi* method of composition. In their view, writing, although it has evolved with time, must retain old mannerisms and dated formulas. Given that most of

our expressions and sayings today have their roots in Arabic, what harm is
there in drawing upon other foreign languages to benefit the literary language and to expand our own? There is no need to limit our imitation to Arabic. (126)

Carefully negotiating his path around Turkish, Mustawfi gives the appearance
of openly embracing any language as a possible source of linguistic renaissance.

As if to give more substance to his conviction of the rich potential of other
languages, Mustawfi continues to translate expressions from disparate
sources. To illustrate the wealth of literary resources available outside Persian,
he mingles Persian poetry and allusions to European literature. When he cites
a sentence from Victor Hugo, for example, he provides the source (1982,
1:318). So meticulous is he in his approach to documenting sources that in
another section of volume 1, he uses an expression he has heard from someone else, but immediately points out he is not certain of its source. The sentence reads: "But Mirza Mahmud passed these last difficult quarter hours of
his life with utmost calm and generosity" (194). Mustawfi then explains in the
footnote that he first heard expression, "last quarter hours," from a Russian
colonel with whom he was conversing in French: "But I do not know whether
the colonel translated this expression from his mother tongue, or the expression is French in origin. In any event, it is not Persian. If the use of translated
idiom is rejected in certain quarters, then this expression will also belong in
their rank. No matter, for soon it will find its place in current Persian usage"
(194). Mustawfi's confidence in the inclusion of this turn of phrase into Persian idiom reflects the efforts that were underway to create Persian equivalents
for objects and institutions newly introduced into Persian. If he sees no harm
in translating an expression and promoting its common usage, it is because a
Persian academy was hard at work officially introducing new words into Persian vocabulary.

Mustawfi's preoccupation with renewal of Persian language is part and
parcel of his reverence for his mother tongue. In his treatment of Persian, he is
very much the explorer delighted with unexpected discoveries he makes at

every turn. He is very enthusiastic about the adoption of colloquial language into modern Persian, which he views as a necessary democratization and a movement away from distinctions between the language of the elite and that of the masses. In a footnote relating a particular usage that has deviated from its origins, Mustawfi once again launches into an argument about the inevitability of linguistic transformations. This time, however, he enhances his usual argument by adding that the language of a country belongs to the entirety of the population and must reflect all levels of usage. If common usage modifies an expression, Mustawfi believes it to be indicative of the fact that the language is moving toward clearer *and* more poetic forms of expression. He ends this footnote with: "Persians are poetic by nature. If the defenders of antiquated writing would permit, our language would become in a very short period of time the sweetest tongue" (1982, 1:279).

So thoroughly convinced is Mustawfi of the need for linguistic innovation that he is occasionally willing to overlook unidiomatic uses of Persian. For instance, when his companion and coworker at the Persian consulate in St. Petersburg, Asad, falls in love and claims "to be in love like a dog," Mustawfi cites him directly and proceeds to justify his friend's incorrect usage:

> In Persian, when one wishes to offend someone, one compares that person to an animal. For instance, he or she eats like a donkey, bellows like a cow, is as small as a mouse, etc. In many instances, humans are also compared to dogs: barks like a dog, pants like a dog, lies like a dog, although dogs do not speak to be able to lie. In other words, this analogy has no basis. . . . In any event, the late Asad Bahadur, who was not raised in Persia and did not know Persian all that well, was under the impression that to give the highest mark was to be compared to a dog. He would repeatedly say in conversation that so and so is in love with such and such a girl like a dog, although dogs are not known for love. The only point of comparison might be the excessive attention lovers give their beloved, but this does not have much currency. (159)

What Mustawfi lays bare here is his attempt to accommodate his friend's eccentric, to say nothing of inaccurate, uses of Persian. He devotes a footnote to this nonexisting turn of phrase whose focus is not so much the linguistic slip itself, but rather the understandable reasons for which it might have been made. The manner in which Mustawfi completes this explanation hints at a desire on his part to allow for this unexpected and uncommon expression to enter Persian idiom. He leaves us with the impression that should this usage gain currency, there would be no logical reason to rule it unfeasible.

What becomes evident in Mustawfi's reflections on Persian, Turkish, Arabic, and French is that his relationship to language is determined not only by his Persian nationalism, to say nothing of ethnocentrism, but also by his encounter with the West. It is in the process of learning French and acquiring fluency in it that Mustawfi finds yet another means of freeing Persian from Turkic domination. Moreover, French comes with an interesting cultural baggage: a history of having carried off a successful social revolution. Mustawfi's desire to import French into Persian goes beyond his perennial search for apt idioms and sayings. In his imagination, French symbolizes the potential for radical cultural and political transformation. To speak French is to gain entry into a realm of boundless possibility for change and into the ethos of modernity.

He is first introduced to French when he enrolls in the newly established *Madrisih-i Siyasi* (School of Politics). Of all the subjects he has to study, he finds himself most inadequate in French. He regrets not having taken advantage of the French tutors who had been employed for his nephews. In an internal monologue, he reflects: "For the next four years, I have to devote every day and night to my studies, especially French that I have to learn one letter of the alphabet at a time, oh my!" (72). He outlines his perseverance at improving his French to the point that he finally catches up with his peer group. At this stage of learning, Mustawfi measures his knowledge of French in relation only to that of the other students at the School. But when he arrives in St. Petersburg in 1904, he becomes conscious of the need for a different level of proficiency in French and its accompanying cultural grammar.

It should be kept in mind that French is the language through which Mustawfi comes to know the West and that, for him, it represents the key to the discovery and understanding of European civilization. In fact, most of his experiences in Russia are filtered through French. For example, when he re-

ceives news of revolutionary activity at home, he decides to translate a history
of the French Revolution for the edification of his compatriots instead of
drawing upon the Russian revolution brewing right in front of his eyes. Because the realities of Russia are only accessible to him through French, he is
not in a position to assess the significance of the revolutionary fervor that
swept Russia in 1905 and was eventually subdued.

There are many interesting instances of his secondhand relationship to
Russian. For instance, he gains insight into the wide gap separating Russian
nobility from the lower classes through his English landlady who speaks
French. The anecdote Mustawfi records in his memoirs concerns a young servant in the employ of his landlady. In order to make the recently employed
peasant more presentable, the landlady gives the young woman money to go
to the baths. The young woman is dumbfounded and inquires: "What is a
bath?" (1982, 2:127). When asked how she had managed to clean herself before coming to St. Petersburg, the servant points out that once or twice a year,
she would wash herself in a stream. Mustawfi ends this anecdote with the landlady's words: " 'What can you expect of someone who has not even heard of a
bath?' " (127). This is not the only occasion on which Mustawfi identifies
with Western Europeans against Russians.

During a visit to Trioki in Russian-occupied Finland, he and his companion, Asad, find themselves with the unusual problem of being turned down by
cab drivers. Eventually they realize that the locals, who have a deep hatred of
the Russian colonizers, are mistaking them for visitors from Russia. The solution Mustawfi and Asad arrive at is to speak Persian to each other as they approach the line of carriages waiting to be hired. This ensures that the driver
would not mistake them for Russians and agree to transport them in his carriage (133–34).

In the Finns' vehement and sustained dislike of Russians, Mustawfi finds
an important indicator of the Russian Empire's internal problems. That after a
hundred and fifty years of Russian occupation the Finns he encounters are not
completely fluent in Russian strikes him as an amazing sign of their resistance,
which he also extends to their attempt to maintain their ethnic "purity": "The
Finns have kept their features fully. It is clear that they have avoided any rela-

tions with Russians" (134). There are echoes of Persian linguistic, racial, and cultural anxieties in Mustawfi's awe for the resilience of the Finns. But also registered in this passage is the prevalence of a broader tendency to see Russian civilization as inferior to the French one or to those of other Western European nations.

For Mustawfi, the most impressive Russians are the nobility who are conversant in Western European languages and whose family trees reach well beyond Russia. Yet he is careful not to specify his preferences and declares that he found Russians to be kind and generous toward strangers (1982, 2:101). The description of his duties as a diplomat and his interactions with members of other embassies obviates the need to distinguish among Russian, French, and Finnish and, instead, enables him to speak of a "European culture" in totalizing terms. For him, this term signifies a high culture best represented at that time by French rules and codes of conduct. The extent to which he takes the supremacy of French language and culture for granted is at least indirectly revealed in his own attitudes toward how French should be spoken.

Mustawfi's dependence on French as the primary medium of access to Europe and things European produces in him a purist attitude. While tolerant of Asad, the coworker, whose Persian is peppered with unidiomatic expressions, Mustawfi shows little understanding toward his compatriots who have not fully mastered French. He has this to say about a Persian official who is given the task of translating a speech delivered by Muzaffar al-Din Shah during his visit to St. Petersburg: "The Shah gave a response in Persian and Muhandis al-Mamalik, who was standing behind him, offered a translation. . . . In my opinion, the translation of the Shah's speech, which was not particularly long in the original, was rather long-winded. I do not know how and under whose supervision this speech had been prepared. It was not *chic*. Moreover, Muhandis al-Mamalik's delivery, even though he was speaking French, had something of a Kashi *accent*" (emphasis added, 1982, 2:155). Mustawfi directly imports the words "chic" and "accent," or *aksan* in his Frenchified Persian, into his text. His frustration with the translator's French is such that, even years after the event, he cannot overcome a desire to switch into French to demonstrate the proper French accent for the occasion. If he inserts French words into his Persian description, it is not to be pretentious by demonstrating his knowledge of French; rather, it indicates that his memory is overwhelmed with the inadequacy of the translator's French. The more Mustawfi delves into his memory of this episode, the more he slips away from Persian into French. What is also highlighted here and in other passages reflecting Mustawfi's views on French is one of the inadvertent outcomes of the linguistic reforms of the Constitutionalist era: "Ironically, it was not long before these early efforts to purify the Persian language from Arabic words fell prey to another extreme, namely, the excessive use of European, mainly French, terms. Perhaps French vocabulary was viewed as an inevitable, and therefore justifiable, vehicle of modernity" (Gheissari 1998, 24).

Mustawfi's passing comment that the translator's French betrayed his native accent of Kashan does not at first appear to hold much significance, but it does hint at a number of Mustawfi's linguistic and cultural obsessions. On one level, Mustawfi seems to suggest that the translator's failure to speak an accentless French is attributable to his never having overcome his regional language and identity. This inability to transcend the local in turn prevents him from learning the standard French of the diplomatic circles. Beyond wishing all Persian representatives to be meticulous in their observation of European manners and customs, Mustawfi translates the mark of an accent into an absence of desire for the language and culture of the other, and ultimately, it forestalls the process of transculturation of which he was an avid proponent.

In order to better grasp the intertwining of linguistic and cultural fluency in Mustawfi's imagination and their crucial role in the reenvisioning of Persian identity in which Mustawfi and many of his contemporaries were engaged, I would like to turn to a specific segment of Mustawfi's memoirs: the state luncheon he attended at the czar's palace in St. Petersburg on January 6, 1905.

Mustawfi originally wrote the description of this event for anonymous publication in a Persian newspaper. The essay turned out to be too long for a newspaper column, but Mustawfi inserts it unchanged in the appropriate section of his memoirs, that is, his arrival in St. Petersburg and the preparations leading up to his formal introduction to the czar and the empresses at a state luncheon on January 6. As Mustawfi explains to his readers, the presentation of new diplomatic appointments to the czar was most often slated for official celebrations like the New Year. Because 1905 had begun with revolutionary turmoil in St. Petersburg, the czar's reception of the diplomatic corps was postponed until January 6. It is interesting that, in the original essay itself, Mustawfi does not mention the nature of the turmoil, nor does he specify that there had been a violent incident in which members of the royal family had barely escaped injury. He inserts the relevant material only after he has presented the piece in its original form. In composing the essay for a newspaper, Mustawfi might have found himself reverting to rules of diplomacy and discretion. As we shall see in his description of the episode, however, a more compelling reason for this absence of historical contextualization is Mustawfi's desire to focus his readers' attention on his own transcultural performance.

Mustawfi was by no means the highest-ranking diplomat at the Persian consulate, nor, as we have already observed, was he the first Persian to set foot outside his homeland. In fact, Mustawfi's generation had extensive contact with the West and diligently recorded its observations for Persian readers. Even the Persian kings who traveled to Europe could not resist writing down their impressions, not foreseeing that their subjects' fascination with life outside Persia would lead to a questioning of their own power. The year 1905, that in which Mustawfi was officially received in St. Petersburg, marks the beginning of a revolutionary period that culminated in the institution of a constitutional monarchy in Persia.

In diametric opposition to the revolution of 1979, the Constitutional Revolution was fueled by an avid curiosity about the West. As the historian Tavakoli-Targhi points out in his comparative study of the two Persian revolutions: "European penetration and intervention in Iranian political economy had begun in the early 19th century, but the negative image of an imperialist and interventionist West was a product of 20th century political experience. While the Western intervention was disliked from early on, the European political and economic system was regarded highly . . . In the Iranian political discourse Europe came to symbolize civilization, enlightenment, knowledge, military and political might" (1988, 170). Mustawfi's attitudes toward Europe are the product of this period of encounters between Persia and the West, but what makes his work stand out is that he does not merely occupy the position of the observer extolling the virtues of European civilization. Rather, he enacts the role of a transcultural Persian by providing a step-by-step illustration of a cultural makeover. As we shall see, the description of the afternoon of January 6, 1905, encapsulates the intense curiosity and effort embedded in the self-transformation so many Persians of this generation wished to achieve. Mustawfi's menu for transmutation is addressed to a generation of Persians who saw alterity as a vehicle for change.

Mustawfi's attitude toward European customs and manners is an extension of his conviction with regard to other languages, that is, that national traits are improved through observation, imitation, and crossbreeding. Imbued with this spirit, he arrives in St. Petersburg highly conscious of his lack of familiarity with European culture: "I confess that I knew nothing of European customs, not even their dress code and table manners. Having heard of some awkward incidents caused by Persian delegates in Europe, I was most eager not to step outside the bounds of good manners. As I knew nothing whatsoever in this area, I had to proceed cautiously. I resolved to approach the matter through careful study in order to avoid adding yet another anecdote to the repertoire of gaucheries committed by uncouth Persians" (114–15). The emphasis he places on the behavior of Persians who had preceded him recalls some colorful chapters of Persian diplomatic history.

Almost exactly a century before him, between the years 1809 and 1810, Mirza Abul Hasan Khan, a Persian envoy to Great Britain, had become the focus of many anecdotes and satirical portrayals, the best known among them James Morier's Hajji Baba novels. Mirza Abul Hasan Khan's indifference to British protocol became the cause of much consternation. When in 1810 the Mirza was asked by the *Morning Post* to express his views on the British way of life, he did not hesitate to offer his candid remarks in a rudimentary English, which nevertheless gave full expression to his disapproval of British social mores. Here is a portion of his letter in which he offers helpful advice on women's participation in evening parties: "I not like such crowd in evening every night—In cold weather not very good—now, hot weather, much too bad. I very much astonish, every day now much hot than before, evening parties much crowd than before. Pretty beautiful ladies come sweat that not very good—I always afraid some old Lady in great crowd come dead, that not very good, and spoil my happiness.—I think old ladies after 85 years not come to evening party that much better.—Why for take so much trouble?" (Qtd. in Wright 1985, 226). Whereas Mirza Abul Hasan Khan shrugs off the uproar his well-intentioned but tactless suggestions cause, Mustawfi does not even venture into European society, let alone express opinions about it, until he has informed himself sufficiently on proper uses of language and rules of conduct. In fact, his description of the luncheon is preceded by details of the long and complex process through which he educated himself in European life and manners:

> I was fortunate in that I had begun my term toward the end of the season for official receptions and had some time to prepare myself for all eventualities. Two other factors came to my rescue: one was a book of manners that fell into my hands. It covered everything from how to hold a knife and fork, how to eat an artichoke, how to deliver speeches at royal dinners, what constitutes proper formal attire, how to leave cards announcing one's visit, what to expect in formal invitations, and how to respond to them. . . . My second stroke of luck was meeting a Persian coworker at the consulate who had been raised in an excellent family in Europe. (115)

Mustawfi's reciting of the table of contents of the book of etiquette echoes his recollection of his first lessons in French. As he had to approach French through the learning of a completely new alphabet, his acculturation is to be achieved through a systematic study of the many rules that, in his imagination, make up European culture.

At the end of the eight months of study and practice, he reports his successful transformation: "I had prepared myself in every way. My spoken French was much perfected. My suit was made by the most renowned tailor in St. Petersburg, my shirt the work of the best in the trade. In a word, I was one of the most dashing, cultivated young men around town and in no way did I trail behind anyone, including officials of the other embassies" (115). Ironically, after all the trouble Mustawfi has taken with his appearance, the day of the banquet he must exchange his European apparel for the official Persian attire. There is a hint of his irritation with having to forgo the display of his mastery of European dress in a description he gives of how he handled himself upon arrival at the palace: "I knew that clinging to your own embassy's delegation was not in the best of manners, especially given the hat we wore those days as part of our formal attire, which had a way of shouting out your nationality, even at a great distance" (116). The hat functions much like the accent of the Persian translator accompanying the Persian king to Russia. It betrays an allegiance Mustawfi does not find appropriate for the occasion of the invitation to the czar's palace. He is so eager to conform to European norms that he sees all visible signs of his Persian identity as a handicap.

This unease with his Persian-style hat pales in comparison with the anxiety Mustawfi encounters at the dining table. His dilemma stems from the single-mindedness with which he devoted himself for eight months to the study and rehearsal of European identity, causing him to neglect the fact that at the banquet he would have to appear as a Persian. Here is Mustawfi's own dramatic revelation of the gap he suddenly discovers between his appearance and what he has learned and is eager to exhibit:

> At the table, the first thing that caught my attention was the beautifully printed menu placed in front of each of us. I had learned in my book of European manners that after such events the guests normally take the menu as a keepsake. Immediately I began worrying about how to transport the menu on my person. My official garb, its buttons, hooks, belt, and sword notwithstanding, did not have a proper pocket. It is true that in those days our formal outfit included a hat and it would have been possible to slip the menu inside the hat and to carry it in the manner of messengers of another time. But the relatively large cardboard menu could not be made to fit into the hollow of the hat without a few risks. The slightest miscalculation could make the cardboard act as a spring and could propel it like a football into the crowd. Moreover, the very attempt to maneuver the menu into the hat in front of

everyone could create another one of those scenes by which Persian officials have made their presence known abroad. (117)

The comical scenes Mustawfi imagines creating betray his immense anxiety about making a fool of himself in his first public and official appearance among Europeans. Speaking about miscalculations and maneuvers, he indicates that he approaches his performance with the rigor and precision of a field marshal.

Befitting this near-military posture, Mustawfi does not give into his sense of panic and, instead, forces himself to remember the numerous other points of etiquette he has fastidiously studied. The most immediately striking among them is the proper use of the printed menu.

He has read in his famous book of manners that guests normally glance at the menu at the end of each course in order to plot their way through the meal more strategically, saving room for the full nine courses by having only small portions of the courses less to their liking. For Mustawfi, however, the usefulness of the menu is subordinated to its status as a prop in yet another stage of his performance:

> The truth is that I was not yet familiar enough with European cuisine to examine the menu for the purposes of planning a course of action pleasing to my palate. But I had read that good table manners dictate that each course be tasted and that not to partake of the food would register as a rebuff to the host. Needless to say, our host was not present at our table. Nevertheless proper manners had to be observed. For this reason, like others, after each course was completed and new sets of plates and cutlery were being placed on the table, I would study the menu. I took this occasion to memorize the names of the courses that appealed to me so that next time I would not merely imitate others, but make some educated choices of my own. (118)

It is not surprising that Mustawfi makes no mention of any of the food served that day. Apart from his scant knowledge of European cuisine at that time, any sensory pleasure he might have experienced is undermined by anxiety at the end of each course when he has to reexamine the menu and be reminded of the challenge before him. Moreover, he has convinced himself that he is not at the luncheon to take pleasure, but rather to please his European audience and present himself as a model of civility and sensibility. The enjoyment of the meal is a luxury he cannot yet afford. Instead, all his energy is devoted to the observation of the proper modes of conduct: "I should point out that, although preoccupied with these thoughts, I did not overlook the two table companions seated on either side of me. I remained engaged in small talk and in no way appeared pensive" (118). The front he presents to his table companions is sharply set against intense internal debates, calculations, and worries. Firmly hidden behind his mask of calm is an extremely distraught and vigilant individual. Even when he appears to have arrived at a solution to his dilemma, he is careful to weigh all the options:

I noticed the Turkish military attaché, who was wearing something similar to what I was wearing, though as his outfit was military it did come furnished with a pocket. I glanced again at the menu and realized that, fortunately, it was too large to fit into that pocket. Then it crossed my mind that his pocket could have been bigger than the regulation size. This possibility worried me and I began to wonder whether I could stash the menu in the back pocket of my uniform. I reexamined the menu and grasped the futility of this option. Even if the pocket itself could accommodate the shape of the menu, its opening was not wide enough. Furthermore, once inserted into the back pocket, the menu would distort the shape of my outfit. This pocket was meant exclusively for gloves. Even our handkerchief had to be placed inside the starched cuffs and not the back pocket where it would bulge and become unsightly. My only remaining option in the matter of the menu was to keep an eye on my Turkish companion and follow his lead. (118)

Mustawfi is not particularly happy to rely on a Turk on a point of European etiquette. His personal prejudices against Turks make him less than confident about the prospects of a Turkish role model: "All the while, I was also keeping an eye on the Turkish official, especially when after each course, like others, he would take the menu off the table to examine. I was particularly anxious that this gentleman, who was not far ahead of us Persians in the knowledge of European manners, would prematurely slip the menu into some compartment of his outfit he had already designated for this purpose. It also crossed my mind that he might not have any interest in keeping the menu as a memento and that all my surveillance would prove pointless" (118).

Mustawfi's apprehension about the image he will be presenting his European counterparts is redoubled because not only will he be seen as an uncouth Persian, he now also runs the risk of being lumped together with all other "Orientals" who have acquired a reputation among Europeans. This anxiety is reflected in an earlier passage in which he ruminates on the possibility of abandoning the menu altogether:

> I could certainly not hold the menu in my hand, especially during the audience with the czar and the empresses. I could just see the protocol officer, draped in blue sash and carrying an ivory-tipped cane, coming forward and asking one of his underlings to remove the menu from me. I was at a loss and had almost resigned myself to leaving the menu behind. But it occurred to me that the Norwegian fellow sitting next to me would wonder how I had become so culturally bereft as to fail to appreciate the beauty of this object. No doubt he would see this as confirmation of the total absence of manners among Orientals and presume that no degree of change could make us equal to our Western counterparts. (117)

In isolation, this passage could be read as an instance of inferiority complex vis-à-vis Europeans, but, in the larger context of Mustawfi's passion for his own culture and language, it points to a more deep-seated desire to represent Persians as sensitive to cultural difference. This entire nerve-racking performance is not so much aimed at transforming himself into a European gentleman as proving that, Persian as he is, he can appreciate and observe the finest nuances of European manners.

Throughout this account, Mustawfi is careful to convey a sense of calm and control to his readers. The description he provides for his compatriots serves a different function from his original performance on January 6, 1905: to illustrate how in an unfamiliar cultural setting adversities of all manner and magnitude can be overcome through ingenuity and common sense. In this spirit, rather than blurting out his immense relief at the meal being over, he says: "Its magnitude notwithstanding, the luncheon finally came to an end" (118). Yet, the resolution to his problem is further delayed when the guests are presented with individual bowls of water with which to wash and tidy up. Having ensured that, like his European counterparts, he is sporting a fashionable à la Kaiser moustache, Mustawfi is on familiar ground. Yet his desire to conform with European norms is once again constrained by his Persian appearance and the Turkish role model he has had to adopt, albeit grudgingly:

> Those dressed in European manner freshened up rather quickly, but the Turk, perhaps because he had eaten too many nuts and was having difficulty dislodging them from between his teeth, took his time. I, who had started my ablutions before him, realized how rash I had been and drew out the drying and curling of my moustache until the Turk had caught up with me. My eyes were riveted on him who now took the menu and lengthwise placed it between his index and middle fingers. Thus giving the menu a concave shape, he slid it smoothly inside his left cuff. The menu was neither too thick to become folded, nor too thin to slide right out. This maneuver struck me as simple enough to be undertaken even by someone not practiced in it. So, as if I had done this a thousand times before, I slipped the menu into my sleeve and got up and left the table with everyone else. (118–19)

There is a sense of pride and satisfaction in the final sentence of this paragraph, although what follows confirms that it is marred by the irony that the credit for ingenuity must go to the Turk.

As if to redress this imbalance, Mustawfi inserts an anecdote that shifts the focus away from his having depended on the Turkish military attaché to his own accomplishment:

It is clear that had I had the intelligence of Avicenna's famous pupil, I would have thought of this solution on my own. The story goes, one day a young man was sent to the baker to bring back hot coals. When the baker loaded his shovel with coals and approached him, he took one look at the boy and shouted: "Boy, you haven't brought a container to put the hot coals in?" Constrained as he was by time, the young man nevertheless thought of a solution. He cupped his hands, dipped them under cold ashes, and coated his palms. He then brought his hands forward and said: "Master baker, here is my container." Well, not everyone can be as smart as this boy. His quick wit so impressed Avicenna, who happened to be in the bakery at the time that he took him on as one of his pupils.

Filled with youthful pride and relieved at having found a way out of my predicament, I was nevertheless not unhappy with myself. (119)

This anecdote, like the dining scene Mustawfi has just described, emphasizes spontaneity and, at first glance, would seem to run against the grain of the preceding narrative. Nowhere in Mustawfi's meticulous and systematic preparations is there room for an uncalculated move, while the problem he confronts requires precisely the spontaneity he has worked so hard to eradicate from his self-presentation to the Europeans at the czar's palace. The anecdote he appends to his descriptions allows him both to get past the prominence the Turkish military attaché has inadvertently acquired in the narrative and, more importantly, to demonstrate his own agility in learning as readily from a Turk as from a European. This makes up for the lack of spontaneity he displays through most of the afternoon and allows Mustawfi to declare his performance at the luncheon a success.

In this light, it is not surprising that Mustawfi's encounter with the czar and the empresses, which was to have been the high point of the day, is mentioned almost as an afterthought: "When the time came for me to be introduced to the czar, my extensive study and rehearsal bore fruit. The presentation proceeded as it should. In fact, I would go further and say that my answers to the questions the empress, the czar's mother, asked me were well chosen and equally well delivered" (119). There is, in fact, no compelling reason for Mustawfi to dwell on his introduction to the czar because it does not represent a challenging aspect of his adjustment to European ways. In his accounts of life in Europe, Mustawfi is much more interested in episodes that focus on the ingenuity required to adapt to new circumstances; his focus is constantly trained on the perceptions Europeans will form of Persians. This is underlined in the sharp contrast he draws between his own behavior on January 6, 1905, and the Persian king's visit to St. Petersburg shortly thereafter.

One the most trying phases of Mustawfi's career coincides with the Persian monarch's visit to St. Petersburg. The personal agonies and embarrassment Mustawfi suffers are even more noticeable in light of the fact that both Persia and Russia are going through the kind of political turmoil worthy of more attention than the conduct of the countries' monarchs.

Although Mustawfi is guarded in his criticism of Muzaffar al-Din Shah's behavior, he does nevertheless point out that the king dozes off during a concert given in his honor by the czar: "The program for the concert was . . . beautifully designed and printed. Everyone in attendance had a copy of the program in hand. In the middle of the concert, his excellency Muzaffar al-Din Shah took a little snooze from which he awoke when the program fell out of his hand. The czar leaned over, picked up the program, and with utmost politeness presented it to his royal guest" (1982, 2:142). Mustawfi's comparison of the behavior of the two heads of state leaves no room for doubt as to whom Mustawfi finds to be living up to his expectations. That neither monarch was particularly successful in his reign does not preoccupy Mustawfi. His primary concern is with visible and tangible marks of royalty and in the case of Muzaffar al-Din Shah, his inability to conform to the standards of his European counterparts. What matters most to him is the execution of a performance crediting Persians with the ability to shuttle back and forth between cultures.

Mustawfi is much less circumspect in his discussion of what he considers to be the worst of Muzaffar al-Din Shah's infractions. On the morning he is due to leave St. Petersburg, the czar arrives at the shah's quarters to bid him farewell. The czar is made to wait, as inquiries reveal that the shah is still asleep. Mustawfi reports that the czar eventually left, but, for Mustawfi, the

czar's departure does not mark the end of this episode. In a paragraph immediately following the summary of the morning's events, he writes: "At ten
o'clock, an hour and a half late, His Majesty, the king of Persia, emerged from
his sleeping quarters. With his entourage, who had been made to wait an hour
and a half, he got into the carriage that had also been made to wait for an hour
and a half in front of the palace, and, an hour and half later than the appointed
time, they boarded the train. Needless to say, the train will reach all its desti-
nations an hour and half later than expected" (146). The repetition of the
length of delay in this passage is a reminder of the number of levels on which
the shah has managed to disrupt the life of the nation hosting him. In order to
stress the extent of the damage caused by the shah's inconsiderate delay,
Mustawfi devotes three other segments of his text to the consequences. Beginning with the carriage drivers and the horses and proceeding to the passengers waiting to board the same train, Mustawfi provides an extensive list of all
those who have been gravely inconvenienced by the shah. In the final section,
he reveals how the entire system of rail transportation was affected for a week
by the shah's lack of concern for protocol (147).

Mustawfi's dwelling on the chain reaction that ensues from the shah's late
start is integral to his view of identity as a performance contingent on circumstances and surroundings. The shah's diplomatic blunder is unforgivable because this was not the only morning on which the czar had come to visit him
at an appointed hour. He is doubly negligent in his overlooking the particular
significance of the morning destined for his departure. In his ineptitude,
Muzaffar al-Din Shah ends up offending not only the czar, but also an entire
nation. The shah disqualifies himself as an equal, worthy of European respect,
and fails to give a proper representation of Persia and his subjects.

If, as the head of his nation, the shah provides an unappealing example,
members of his entourage do little to correct the impressions left by the shah.
During the same royal visit, Mustawfi mentions, the shah's entourage had not
only not received any training in how to kiss the hand of the empress, they
were incapable of following the example of those among them who were informed on this point of etiquette. Mustawfi watches in horror as certain members of the Persian delegation plant rather loud and sloppy kisses on the

empress's hand, ensuring that their foreheads touch the back of her hand. This last maneuver, adopted from the manner of greeting a Persian clergyman, is particularly shocking to Mustawfi: "I was praying that at least their foreheads not be sweaty. Otherwise, although the empress would be the only one in the know, to this already unseemly display would be added a deeper level of filth" (138–39). In this passage Mustawfi gives voice to one of the central tenets of his doctrine of transculturation: the necessity of adopting an appearance that makes it possible to pass for someone of a different nationality. This is not to say that he is solely concerned with the external facets of a culture, but rather that he intuits the first means of breaking through a cultural barrier to consist of playing the role well enough to be mistaken for a native. The shah and some members of his entourage do not even grasp the need for playing according to different rules.

Mustawfi's reasons for pitting the dining scene of January 6, 1905, against events that took place during Muzaffar al-Din Shah's official visit are inextricably interwoven with his notion of cultural adaptation. The description of his own behavior at the czar's banquet shows him to be at an earlier stage of his experience of other cultures. At the luncheon, he is not particularly keen to own up to being a Persian. The lesson he learns that day is that it is not necessary for him to exchange one identity for another. After all, he is not interested in denying his Persian heritage or discarding it. In other words, the point is not for him to be either European or Persian, but rather to internalize the gap between the two and know *how* and, even more importantly, *when* to bridge them.

An anecdote he relates from his visit to London gives us an illustration of the relationship to alterity Mustawfi develops later in the course of his stay in Europe. There are many obvious parallels between the luncheon in St. Petersburg and the audience in Buckingham Palace. This episode also revolves around dress code and the proper observance of rules of etiquette.

When the Persian delegation of which Mustawfi is a member is waiting in an antechamber to be received by the British monarch, Mustawfi observes that he and his compatriots have gloves on their left hands, but not their right hands. Normally not wearing a glove on their right hand would be in full conformity with the protocol for shaking hands with the king. But it dawns on Mustawfi that the king's outfit might be different and require long gloves in which case he would be wearing both gloves. Mustawfi reasons with himself that, were this to be the case, extending their ungloved right hand to the king would not be acceptable. He approaches Mr. Parker, an employee of the foreign ministry who has been appointed to accompany the visiting Persians, and asks: "Is His Majesty wearing a military uniform today, or is he wearing something that includes gloves?" (1982, 2:194). It is what unfolds at this point and the manner in which Mustawfi responds to it that deserves close attention:

He did not answer me. Because I did not want him to wander about the room in order to investigate and come back with an answer, I let the matter go. But Parker, who had intuited my purpose, approached General Eslid[2] and inquired with him. The general was not aware what the king would be wearing, but strolled over to the chief protocol officer and asked him. The protocol officer thought things over a bit and then headed toward the king's chambers. Parker, who had rejoined us immediately, did not behave as though he had spoken to the general for the sole purpose of finding an answer to my question. He continued to speak with us in the same calm fashion as before. . . . But I had noted that it was my question that had prompted all this movement in the room. After a few minutes, the protocol officer returned and passed by the general . . .

I saw Parker inch toward the general, who was also headed toward Parker. They exchanged a couple of words and continued their separate ways. A minute later, Parker turned to me and said: "Did you ask me a question? I believe I may have neglected to provide you with an answer in the course of our conversation." I, in turn, acted as if I had not noticed any of them coming and going and said: "I do not seem to remember what it was." He replied: "Concerning the king's gloves." I exclaimed: "Oh, yes. I would be most grateful if you could share with me any information you might have on

2. This is the spelling I have reconstructed from Mustawfi's Persian transliteration. The correct spelling of the general's name might well be different.

this point." To which he responded: "Yes, what the king is wearing today requires him to have a glove on his right hand as well." (194–95)

In this scene, Mustawfi and Parker are on equal footing both in their knowledge of protocol and in their calm and controlled approach to the resolution of what they see as a potential breach of etiquette. On this occasion, Mustawfi can share his concerns with the highest-ranking among the British courtiers. Moreover, it is now *he* who becomes the role model.

After Parker has provided him with the necessary information, Mustawfi, has to find a way of communicating it to the Persian ambassador: "I wondered how to let the ambassador in on this information. I could not think of anything other than putting the glove on my right hand, which I proceeded to do, as I made a big show of getting my fingers into the glove. Mushir al-Mulk caught on and, because he knew normally I would not be ostentatiously fidgeting with my fingers, he realized he had to wear the glove on his right hand" (195). Remarkably it is the ambassador, not Mustawfi, who is called in for the private audience with the king. But Mustawfi's role is not any less crucial in the success of the audience. What saves the day is Mustawfi's ability to see the situation from both the perspective of the Persian diplomat and that of the British courtiers. Mustawfi's pride stems from the fact that in this particular situation the Persian and the British are on equal footing and mirror each other's anxiety about self-representation. In the space of this "contact zone," the Persian and the British can be observed in a relation of mutual influence. Both have to grapple with how they are seen, and they vie with each other for the smoothest possible performance.

Mustawfi's apprehensions about codes of dress and conduct, as I indicated at the beginning of this chapter, do not translate into a servile acceptance of European plans for Persia. In fact, he is highly suspicious of economic and trade overtures made to Persia, which he sees as thinly veiled disguises for larger imperialist designs. In the third volume of his memoirs, he reproduces a letter in which he lists his numerous objections to a proposed Anglo-Persian treaty. Among its many potential detrimental effects, he cites a gradual erosion of Persian culture and language. He points to other nations in the East who have suffered a loss of their culture through European colonization:

> The propagation of the language of the conqueror in a nation and its perfect imitation is natural among human beings. This is particularly true of Persians, whose inherent intelligence, natural literary leanings, and instinct to adapt have demonstrated in the course of history that they cannot remain impartial to the language of conquerors. Once Persian is no longer the medium of social interaction and advancement, it will lose its significance. No one will be interested in studying its literature and, consequently, Persian will lose its literary flourish and be reduced to a mere accent locals employ for basic necessities. Do not give us the example of East Indians and Egyptians. Indians do not have a particularly remarkable literary talent. If English has not replaced the native language, the native tongue has not made much progress either. (1982, 3:110)

It is paradoxical that while invoking the example of India, Mustawfi glosses over the Persian cultural domination of India and proceeds to fault Indians for failing to produce any Persian writers of note. In fact, he sees the absence of Persian writers in India as a side effect of British colonization. His focus is so exclusively turned to Persian national identity that he does not catch his own contradictions and sinks even deeper into grand essentializations on the nature of Egyptians: "As for Egyptians, the only reason they have not surrendered to English, but only slightly mingled their own language with it, is that they are stubborn by nature. The pliability and quickness of Persian wit are radically different from the inflexible and harsh nature of the Arabs" (110). The most remarkable aspect of this passage is that Mustawfi's assessment of the degree and extent of his compatriots' cultural flexibility is based on his own performance in his encounters with other languages and cultures. If he cannot resist adopting French idioms and making himself over to look like a young European man, he assumes all Persians will succumb to the lure of a new identity. Underlying Mustawfi's pronouncements is a peculiar tension between the desire to imitate European ways and the fear of being overwhelmed by European norms.

The interplay of this desire and fear produces an interesting and productive blend of national pride and an immense curiosity about Europe. Although he is careful not to be swept away by either of these emotions, he cannot always maintain a clear line of demarcation between what constitutes the self and the other; as he is learning about Europe, he is also adapting his notion of Persian national traits. The description of his life is, in fact, itself a record of the shifting of the boundaries between the self and the other. The meticulous care with which Mustawfi documents the offices and practices of the Qajar era is a testimony to his role as a curator of a culture in transition. His preservation of the past is double-edged. On the one hand, he wants to maintain a record of the practices and customs of his forefathers. On the other, his cultural history becomes a touchstone against which to observe the transformations that have taken place.

The extent to which this attitude pervades the Persian imagination at this time is reflected in a lead article of the new series of the influential Persian journal *Kavih,* published in Berlin. Hasan Taqizadih, who urges three crucial steps upon his compatriots, authors the piece, inaugurating the new series on January 22, 1920:

> First, the adoption and promotion, without condition or reservation, of European civilization, absolute submission to Europe, and the assimilation of the culture, customs, practices, organization, sciences, arts, life, and the whole attitude of Europe, without any exception save language . . .
>
> Secondly, a sedulous attention to the preservation of the Persian language and literature, and the development, extension, and popularization thereof.
>
> Thirdly, the diffusion of European sciences, and a general advance in founding colleges, promoting public instruction. (Qtd. in Browne 1959, 486)

Taqizadih was to later qualify his zeal for adoption of European civilization, and, as Mohammad 'Ali Eslami-Nodushan has pointed out, these remarks are not representative of the whole of Taqizadih's intellectual career (1969, 533). Nevertheless they encapsulate the spirit that moved so many Persian intellectuals of this era to look outside the borders of their country for means of reconfiguring their cultural and national identity. As Marie Louise Pratt has argued, such crossing of cultural currents do not happen within simple binary frameworks, with one culture or language completely dominating the other. Instead, they revolve around contact zones out of which emerge particular transcultural experiences (1992, 7).

Mustawfi's life history is the best example of this type of experiment with shifting and redrawing boundaries. As a transcultural Persian he represents the history of a crucial era in Persian culture. Dressing up as a European, adopting the proper accent in his spoken French, and learning the minute details of social etiquette are all rehearsals for the ultimate performance he has to deliver on his return to Persia: to reform Persian identity from within.

It is significant that Mustawfi's European sojourn occupies the midsection of his autobiography. His encounter with Europe, unlike Mu'in al-Saltanah's, does not mark the end of his narrative because the emphasis is no longer exclusively on the marvels of the West. For Mustawfi and his generation, much more crucial is the way in which knowledge and insight acquired outside Persia can refashion the country, its image, and identity.

Like the first famous Persian cultural cross-dresser, Uruch Beg, Mustawfi is fascinated with the potential offered up by discovering all that lies beyond Persia. What distinguishes the seventeenth-century convert from the nineteenth-century diplomat is that Mustawfi has full license to carry his new wardrobe back to his native Persia and use it to stage new identities for the benefit of a home audience. But in this process, his Persian audiences are not passive bystanders. Taking their cues from Mustawfi, they too realize that, for their self-transformations, they have a large menu to choose from. As Mustawfi's own example demonstrates, this approach to reform requires a fine balance between instances of individuality and communal identification. The attempt to strike such a balance is at the heart of Mustawfi's presentation of his life. He begins with a descriptive history, imbues it with his personal experiences, which he in turn places within a significant stage of transition in his country. In this sense, his personal life history is inseparable from this particular historical moment.

It is not by chance that the most personal and confessional moments of his memoir turn out to be those in which he has to negotiate a careful path between his culture and others he encounters in the course of his stay in Europe. For instance, he construed the description of his psychological anguish at the luncheon hosted by the czar to be a far more compelling read for his compatriots than any other detail pertaining to his marriage, relationships, and family life. It is against the image of a panic-stricken Mustawfi, pretending to be in complete control, that we are meant to read the remainder of his work. That episode is etched onto his memory and forms the core of the balancing act, which is his memoirs.

4

An Armchair Traveler's Journeys Around the Self

All the European histories and novels that my teacher had read to me, all his descriptions of the world's beautiful cities (accompanied by the reminder, 'The world is not confined to Tehran!') made me long desperately for Europe,"[1] reads the penultimate sentence of Taj al-Saltanah's unfinished memoirs, assumed to have been written in 1914 (1993, 310).[2] This opposition between Tehran, whose geographical and social boundaries define Taj al-Saltanah's existence, and European cities she never saw with her own eyes, captures the mood of her imaginary journeys. Unlike Uruch Beg, Mu'in al-Saltanah, and Mustawfi, Taj al-Saltanah's encounter with the West was confined to the realm of books and hearsay. Frustrating as this absence of concrete reality may have been, it enabled her to engage even more imaginatively with what she read and heard about the West. This meant that sometimes she created fictions of life in the West, which she either held up as perfect models or

---

1. In my analysis, I will cite primarily from Anna Vanzan and Amin Neshati's English translation entitled *Crowning Anguish*. I will make references to the original Persian edited by Mansoureh Ettehadieh and Cyrus Sadounian. For instance, in the passage I have cited, the word *divanihvar* in Persian is translated as "desperately." Embedded in the Persian word is *divanih*, mad, which would suggest "madly" as a closer rendition of the original.

2. On the issue of dating the manuscript, see Afsaneh Najmabadi's "A Different Voice: Taj os-Saltaneh" (1990).

denounced for their inadequacies. But more interesting than her attitudes toward European civilization is the manner in which she found reflections of herself in its mirror and wrote about the *images* of the self she saw emerging through her journeys of the mind.

The contradictory and fractured nature of Taj al-Saltanah's text reflect the paradoxes of the discourses of modernity sweeping Persia at the time. As Meyda Yeğenoğlu has demonstrated in *Colonial Fantasies,* through the drive to modernization "the imperial divide was reproduced *within* the Third World and hence sustained the legacies of Eurocentric thought. The Orientalization of the Orient can be traced back to the ways in which such a fundamental divide took over the discourse of the indigenous elite" (1998, 133). The inherent subordination of women in discourses that replicated themselves in nations such as Persia was, in Yeğenoğlu's words, a legacy of the "grand narrative of the Enlightenment [that] relied on the intrinsic and implicit linkage established between reason, individuality, and masculinity" (106). Afsaneh Najmabadi situates this same logic within Persian modernity:

Concepts central to imagining and constructing modern Iran were envisaged in terms related to concepts of femininity and masculinity. Nation/*millat,* for instance, was largely conceptualized as a brotherhood—at least until the first decade of the twentieth century when women began to claim their space as sisters-in-the-nation. The modern notion of *vatan* (homeland), on the other hand, was envisaged as female—a beloved or mother. Closely linked to the maleness of *millat* and femaleness of *vatan* was the multiple load of the concept of *namus* (honor) in this period. The idea shifted between the purity *(ismat)* of woman and the integrity of the nation, and both were constituted as subjects of male responsibility and protection; sexual and national honor constantly slipped back and forth in the literature of this time.

The gendered construction of such central notions of modernity has in turn had significant political consequences for how the changes in notions of gender, and in particular womanhood, were articulated in the emergence of Iranian modernity. To have envisaged the homeland as a female body, whose purity constituted male honor and was in need of male protection, created a

discursive space within which woman as citizen landed in a domain of conflict, at once claiming purity, yet subject to male protection. (1996, 108)

Taj al-Saltanah's text is written over this same conflicted terrain. Her self-
portrait articulates tensions, vacillating between a self-valorization and a self-
loathing that culminates in a rupture she describes at the end of her memoirs:
"The whole person benefits from knowledge, like most people; I suffered a
loss for having knowledge. Bereft of any basic understanding of the world, of
life and humanity, I consequently adhered to no set of beliefs, and neither depended on anyone nor feared anyone" (310). Encapsulated in these sentences
is the problematic that haunts Taj al-Saltanah's life writing as well as the discourse of Persian modernity: the difficult integration of the new knowledge,
which she also describes as enlightenment, and a sense of "completeness,"
ruptured by that enlightenment. The divided self, although embodying a new
national identity, Persianness, is equally caught in uneasy alignments of gender and nation. The distinction Taj al-Saltanah makes between herself and
those who are *kamil,* complete or whole, affects her relationship with women,
particularly her mother, who stands in for the failures of traditional female upbringing. The psychological anguish that pervades her work is rooted both in
the process of self-discovery the writing of her memoirs initiated and in the attempt to bridge the gaps caused by the competing demands of old and new
notions of female identity.

My reading of Taj al-Saltanah's memoirs will attempt to move beyond the
binarism of Persia and the West many scholars have already noted and analyzed. For instance Farzaneh Milani writes: "when Taj-o Saltanah cannot pinpoint a specific culprit, she blames all the ills and malaise of her personal life
on the overvalued/devalued, idealized/demonized West" (1987, 191). In a
similar vein, 'Abbas Amanat finds Taj al-Saltanah's inner turmoils coinciding
with her introduction to Western concepts. In his introduction to the English
translation, he provides this reading of her attempts at suicide:

Though she does not elaborate on the circumstances of her three suicide attempts, they were no doubt, symptoms of her inner crisis. Her adopting the

European mode of dress, abandoning regular prayer and other devotional acts, and above all unveiling herself in public—not to mention her uninhibited socializing—were enough to confirm her husband's suspicions of unfaithfulness. But more distressing for Taj, these changes seem to have stirred in her a crisis of faith, a sense of guilt, as she began to move away from an innocent "God-fearing world of damnation" and "torments of hell" to a world of rational causality and secular tenets. (1993, 60)

There is no doubt that, as Afsaneh Najmabadi argues, "Taj os-Saltaneh's memoirs are striking for their deep-seated tensions and intense contradictions, apparent on virtually every page" (1990, 29) and that these tensions can be directly or indirectly linked to what she read and heard about life in Europe and North America. My own analysis will shift the ground to an understanding of gaps, factual errors, and contradictions of Taj al-Saltanah's text as integral to her self-perception and self-representation. I place Taj al-Saltanah's memoirs among travel narratives and memoirs that center around Persians' lives in the West precisely because her writing emerges out of an arena, albeit textual and imaginative, of cultural contact and conflict. The ever-shifting paths along which the narrative voice takes us is indicative of the unevenness of the terrain crisscrossed by this armchair traveler. The impossibility of reconstructing fully the stages along which she traveled is a befitting reminder of the missing parts of this Persian princess's story.

On the most immediate level, an exact catalogue of her readings cannot be reconstructed. In his extensive introduction, 'Abbas Amanat provides a general outline of her library: "Taj's knowledge of the West was in part based on . . . translations of popular romances, European histories and geographies, newspaper articles on international affairs, and possibly even Christian polemical literature" (61). The effort to arrive at a precise list of Taj al-Saltanah's readings ultimately leads to conjectures and broad sketches. For instance, in her memoirs she mentions Jean-Jacques Rousseau and Victor Hugo by name, although, as indicated by Amanat (62), neither writer had yet been translated into Persian in 1914. Because the date by which she began her French lessons under the mentorship of a relative cannot be fixed, it is even more difficult to assume that she would have read the French writers in the original. The tone of Taj al-Saltanah's memoirs makes it tempting to presume that she was familiar with Rousseau's autobiographical works. But any possible affinity she might have had with Rousseau cannot be accurately traced and validated.

Beyond this problem of documenting sources, there are too many loose ends in Taj al-Saltanah's narrative to be resolved through establishing the exact nature of her readings. Is the effort to anchor her text in her library of Western texts not overdetermined by conditions Sidonie Smith addresses in her critique of autobiography? "[T]he cultural injunction to be deep, unified, coherent, autonomous 'self' produces necessary failure, for the autobiographical subject is amnesiac, incoherent, heterogeneous, interactive. In that very failure lies the fascination of autobiographical storytelling as performativity" (1998, 110). This notion of performativity offers a different means of reading Taj al-Saltanah's work. In the tug-of-war to establish herself as both isolated from and part of a community we can detect the competing discursive demands in which Taj al-Saltanah's concept of self was imbricated. Following Anne Goldman's suggestion, we can find a way out of this apparent bipolarity: "Rather than fix the subject of a given text as either illustrative of a privileged self, distinguished from others in bold relief, or as an example of the 'we' that is metonymic of a collective, identity might more effectively be appraised with reference to a continuum" (1998, 288). The continuum along which the different selves Taj al-Saltanah's narrative manifest themselves spans a period of rapid cultural transformation that gave rise to the formulation of a Persian national identity and new inscriptions of gender in the discourse of nation. In Mustawfi's accounts, we have already seen how alterity functions as a means of grappling with reconfigurations of Persia and Persians. But in Taj al-Saltanah's writing, the broader narratives of national character are inseparable from the vexed questions of gender identity. Taj al-Saltanah's writing reveals the fissures and contradictions in the ways in which Persia was imagined as a modern nation. The control and the confidence of Mustawfi's narrative are replaced in Taj al-Saltanah's accounts by admissions of alienation and fragmentation.

Interestingly, Taj al-Saltanah represents her childhood as already marked by alienation. Describing the jealousy her engagement at the age of eight provoked in her father's young protégé, 'Aziz al-Sultan, and her own mimicking of the young man's self-centered behavior, she observes "although I had grown up harsh and cold, yet sometimes I acted in an impulsive and mercurial way, which I regretted almost immediately. I was not so dull-witted as to deny my faults. Here my greatest shortcoming was that I understood what I was doing and did it deliberately. That is why when I think about it, I see that I am somewhat out of my mind, and I marvel not a little at myself" (152–53). Taj al-Saltanah attributes her sudden attraction to 'Aziz al-Sultan to the lavish attention her father bestowed upon the spoiled young man. Given her love for her father, there is no doubt that, by mirroring 'Aziz al-Sultan's temperamental ways, Taj al-Saltanah was vying for affection. As she reveals, her relationship to her parents was at best strained. She did not feel particularly loved by her mother. In fact, as we shall see later, she felt deprived of maternal love. In contrast, she idolized her father and believed herself to be one of his favorites. It is not surprising then that she becomes cantankerous when, at her own engagement party, she finds her father's attention diverted away from her. What is unexpected is the link she makes between this day's events and the origins of her internal fragmentation: "It seems that this experience created a second self within me which I still possess. Not only in childhood, but even today—when I have a reputation for being sensible and ethical and civilized—this shortcoming remains with me" (153). The word for self in the original is *akhlaq-i sanavy,* literally, "a second nature." The sense created here is of a second strain running through the composition of her personality.

Taj al-Saltanah's description of her personality aligns it along two poles of "ethical and civilized" and "mercurial" behavior. The one pole requires conformity with standards, the other breaks with norms. The rebel is never too far away from the conformist in her. The constant, to say nothing of the restless, shuttling between these two poles is at the very core of Taj al-Saltanah's image of herself, in which she cannot reconcile the competing demands of seeking self-fulfillment and becoming an enlightened, educated, and self-sacrificing woman and mother. Because the two expectations do not mesh, she declares: "What I can say about myself is that I was not raised well, though I was quite educable. That is why today I feel ashamed, and find myself demeaned and disconsolate" (154). This admission that flaws she finds in herself are inherent to the method of educating, further elucidated in her discussion of the notion of motherhood, is a product of the process of self-discovery reflected in the opening passage of the memoirs.

The scene in which she places herself is initially marked by a darkness and gloom: "It was Thursday evening, the last day of Rab'I, 7 Aquarius 1332 [27 February 1914]. The afternoon was dark and overcast, gloomy as my reveries. Sitting in a half-lit room, I was busily occupied in painting. Outside it was snowing heavily, and no sound was heard except the whiffling of the wind. A despondent silence and stagnation, heightened by the dim red glow radiating from the heater, enveloped me" (107). The exact date she assigns this moment is strikingly set against a sense of time being suspended in the remainder of the passage. Not only are her surroundings steeped in darkness, she is also almost completely cut off from any sound that would confirm other human existence. The only signs of continuation of life are associated with natural phenomena: the wind and the snow. It is interesting to note that even in this moment of isolation, the narrator retains a heightened awareness of the workings of nature. Read in light of Taj al-Saltanah's revelations in the last pages of her memoirs, "as I progressed in my studies day by day, my irreligiosity grew, until I was a complete naturalist myself" (309), her sensitivity to nature foregrounds her belief in the inextricable bond between nature and reason: "After forsaking prayers, I repudiated all religions and beliefs as invalid, arguing, 'Thunder is thunder and lightning is lightning. The tree is exactly as it appears, and so is a human' " (309). Ironically, the simplicity and straightforwardness she attributes to all that is "natural" proves most illusory in her attempt to understand one human life, her own. What she uncovers, beginning with the opening passage of her life history, is that a human being is not necessarily exactly as she appears.

If she gives her own senses and her cognizance of nature prominence in the first lines of her text, it is to single out the subject of her inquiry. To this end, all indications of human activity are temporarily erased and we see only her, "busily occupied in painting." We discover in the next paragraph that the painting in which she appears to be so absorbed is that of a "young woman's face," but that it too fails to capture her full attention, or at least to calm her senses. She describes her brush strokes as "clumsy and haphazard." The original wording translates into "unself-conscious and flawed," reinforcing the narrator's agitation. She appears to be far removed from the movements of her paintbrush, an impression confirmed in her recognition that the image she produces is flawed.

Apart from a marker of the narrator's self-absorption—even the sole source of light in the room is focused on her and "envelops" her—the opening passage of the memoirs also indicates a symbolic attempt to bring herself out of the shadows. This is also conveyed in the narrator's working, however haphazardly, at a painting. The careless brush strokes tell us of a desire to put together a portrait, or to find a means of articulating that which is drawing the narrator deeper within herself. The inner self is so vividly set against all that lies beyond her reveries that we long for the oppressive silence and obscurity to be lifted. This is precisely the drama staged in the first paragraph of the text. In the next paragraph, our anticipation is rewarded.

She now reveals that all along she was being observed by "a melancholic youth who sat behind in an armchair." The presence of the young man allows the preoccupied narrator to be engaged in a dialogue: "Startled by his totally unexpected voice—for I had thought I was alone—I twitched involuntarily and cried, 'Ah, Solayman, were you here all this time?' " (107). Because this interlocutor's mood matches that of the narrator, as if to confirm his melancholia, "From time to time he heaved a doleful sigh," the atmosphere of the scene is not radically disrupted. The harmony between her companion's mood and her own, moreover, serves a secondary purpose of not completely overshadowing Taj al-Saltanah's subjectivity. As it is the conversation between the two that instigates the writing of the memoirs, it gives us a glimpse of Taj al-Saltanah's intellectual independence and creative impulse. The dialogue also makes possible verbalization of her innermost thoughts and provides another means of emergence out of the shadows.

This engagement with another, who is a soul mate, friend, and mentor, marks a transition from the visual to the verbal. The intensity of her descriptions has been so far focused on the play of light and shadows, over and above the fact that she herself is busy painting a portrait. This visual focus now gives way to a verbal prowess that confirms, on another level, the strength and range of the narrator's faculties.

As a means of overcoming her melancholia, Solayman counsels Taj al-Saltanah: "When you feel a pensive mood coming on, it would be better if you occupied yourself with enlivening conversation, or walked outside to admire nature, or read some historical book" (107). The first of Solayman's suggestions is already proven futile insofar as we have taken note of the fact that Taj al-Saltanah was sitting in the same room with him and was still startled by the sound of his voice.

Solayman's second recommendation has also been implicitly discounted in the initial passages of the memoirs. Even in her most meditative state of mind, Taj al-Saltanah is keenly aware of that which is happening in nature. More importantly, this sensitivity to natural phenomena does not prove capable of drawing her out of her self-absorption. If anything, the gloominess of the day mirrors and confirms her own sense of desolation.

As for Solayman's recommendation that she occupy herself with reading history, Taj al-Saltanah responds with indignation: "With a bitter smile on my lips I let out a cry impulsively and said, 'O my dear teacher and cousin! My past and present life excites both wonder and anguish, and you expect me to be interested in another's tale? Isn't the review of one's personal history the best undertaking in the world?' " (108). Taj al-Saltanah's reaction is not simply prompted by the implied offense she has taken at the suggestion that her life does not offer sufficient material for study and observation. This foregrounding of herself echoes the opening scene of the memoirs and directs all attention to the speaker. The rhetorical nature of the series of questions she asks Solayman provides a strategic transition into her life history. But there is even more at stake in what appears to be a pretext to launch into her own story.

The question with which this passage ends goes beyond Taj al-Saltanah's life and makes a statement about the significance of individual life histories. The contestatory tone she adopts is, at least partially, aimed at correcting Persian cultural prejudice against the telling of ordinary lives. Although, as the daughter of Nasir al-Din Shah, she is not exactly ordinary, her being a woman, who has spent a good deal of her life in seclusion, does militate against the assumption of a life eventful enough to merit being written about. Bundled into this defensiveness is Taj al-Saltanah's conviction, most probably acquired through her readings of European literature, that much can be learned from the lives of individuals.

When she later writes, "I wish I were a competent writer like Victor Hugo or Monsieur Rousseau and could write this history in sweet and delightful language. Alas, I can write but simply and poorly" (134), she acknowledges some of her possible sources of inspiration. But, the tone of modesty aside, in writing her own history she blends elements of romantic autobiography, in the style inaugurated by Rousseau's *Confessions,* with the didactic aspect of the Persian tradition of biography. The hybrid form of her project becomes evident in a reply she gives to her mentor's dismissive claim: " 'Ah, but I don't consider the ups and downs of individual experience as history.' " She drops her earlier defense of the importance of coming to terms with one's life, however ordinary, and insists upon the grand proportions of her own life: " 'The story of my life is so weighty and replete with difficult situations that I couldn't finish recounting it even if I spent every hour of an entire year. Besides, it alternates so rapidly between sorrow and laughter that it's bound to perplex the listener' " (108). This implies a recognition on the part of the narrator that to present a personal history to Persian readers requires justification. The opening segment ends with renewed acknowledgment that her life history will serve an end: "Now I begin the story of my life, thereby earning this strange young man's eternal gratitude. At the same time, in reviewing my past, I record both my sufferings and my good fortune and happiness" (109). In other words, she writes primarily to please someone whose presence, at the beginning of this narrative, she admits, in her preoccupation, she barely noticed. The best undertaking in the world, "the review of one's history," is now complemented by a personal and moral obligation.

The paradoxical position she takes on the inherent appeal of her autobiography and its telling having been prompted by the debt she felt she owed Solayman is further reinforced in her inclusion of a brief sketch of her mentor's life history in the frame story. The discussion between Taj al-Saltanah and Solayman having ended with her promise to him that she will write down her story, she adds: "And here I think it appropriate to describe briefly this teacher of mine and introduce him properly before I proceed to tell my story" (108). The outlines of the young man's life offer only a few tantalizing details at once confirming that a seemingly simple life conceals much that can be learned through narration and analysis and also ensuring that the ups and downs of his life do not distract us from the central story of Taj al-Saltanah's own life.

Taj al-Saltanah's description of the young man's life lays bare the broad outlines of the narration of her own. What stands out in her depiction of her mentor is a concern with a balance between descriptions of his physical appearance and his less visible characteristics. Having pointed out the twists and turns of his course of education, his passions, and artistic preoccupations, she writes:

> But enough said about his character. Now I must say something about his appearance. He has an honest, agreeable face with large dark eyes expressive of a pensive temperament. His cheeks are sunken, his skin almost sallow, and his nose like an eagle's beak. Looking at him I am reminded of one of the histories of France in which I had read about Prince de Condé's family, whose noses were always compared to eagles' beaks. He is very gentle and calm— humble and affable toward his inferiors, and amiably disposed toward his fellow mystics. Such are my teacher's appearance and demeanor. (109)

Although she introduces this section with a declaration that she will now replace a presentation of her mentor's character with that of his appearance, she quickly forgets her resolve and demonstrates that his physical characteristics cannot be read in isolation from his gentle temperament. Even his sunken cheeks, his sallow complexion, and his hooked nose enhance inner qualities, implying an intertwining of nature and upbringing.

By likening his nose to the Prince de Condé's, she gently presses the presentation away from his less pleasing physical features and, at the same time, she places him in a gallery of notables not merely known to Persians. In the preceding paragraph, she compares him to Don Quixote: "at the age of eighteen or nineteen he had conceived a fanciful love for someone and adopted the mannerisms of the famous Don Quixote" (109). It is interesting that she looks to European figures, fictional and real, for points of comparison. She would have been familiar with a good many legendary Persians with hooked noses or a reputation for "fanciful love." This is not just a case of showing off her readings in European literature and history. The intrusion of the European names and faces marks an attempt to move away from the cultural over-valorization of physical beauty in which Taj al-Saltanah's narrative is repeatedly entangled.

The pages she devotes to the enumeration of physical attributes, mostly her own, bear witness to an internalization of values that couple female identity with visible marks of beauty. The emphasis on the visible and the need to be visible reflect also the growing debates about veiling as a symbol of women's exclusion from full participation in the creation of a modern Persia. Siding with the reformist movements of the times, Taj al-Saltanah links her personal enlightenment and adoption of a European mode of dress: "My first act was to change my mode of dress. I began to dress in the European style, my head bare, while women in Persia still dressed according to the old style" (309). As Yeğenoğlu argues, this particular conjunction is part of the colonial legacy: "The project of liberating the Oriental woman through unveiling her is inseparable from the mechanism of a subjectifying gaze that is supported by the desire to know her. The visual/scopic drive implicit in all representation is brought out with particular intensity in the field of colonial power" (1998, 110). The transmission of this scopic regime to the Persian elite is confirmed in Taj al-Saltanah's own father's passion for photography. Among his favorite subjects were the women of his harem. According to 'Abbas Amanat, the camera became something of a weapon in Nasir al-Din Shah's hands: "As an amateur photographer, Naser al-Din had a knack for capturing his wives in dull poses, as though he was settling many grudges with them" (39). Amanat provides this description of the images captured by Nasir al-Din Shah: "A combination of starched mini-skirts and white tights, apparently a bizarre mixture of the Persian *shelita* and the Parisian ballerinas' tutu, blouses revealing of large breasts, heavy make-up on flabby cheeks, and artificially bridged eyebrows, blackened with silver nitrate, completed the appearance of a Naseri woman" (39). Amanat's own dislike of the appearance of the female subjects notwithstanding, his description reveals the Shah's panoptical vision, particularly vis-à-vis women. Coupled with an economy of power and desire that allowed him to constantly choose new wives from among the most "beautiful" women, the gaze of the monarch set criteria for female beauty and desirability.

Taj al-Saltanah's own ways of seeing are affected by the standards against which women of her class and status were judged. Her gaze is also informed by her "naturalist" beliefs that assume physical traits to be transparent indicators of character, class, and education. When her views run into contradictions, she sets up exceptions to her constructs.

Nowhere is this tension more evident than in Taj al-Saltanah's description of her black nanny. She devotes a long passage to the description of her nanny's physical appearance:

> About forty or forty-five years of age, of average height, this woman had a very dark face with large eyes. She was generally reticent, but on the few occasions that she did speak her speech was crude and harsh. This dear nanny of mine, having also brought up my mother, had risen to the rank of "Matron Nanny". . . . She was very affectionate to me and very formal and serious with others. I had grown so accustomed to her presence that, despite her fearsome looks and dreadful physique, if she was parted from me for a day, I cried the entire time and nothing could console me. I never left her side, and there was no remedy for being apart from her. Thus it is that, to this day, in memory of my beloved nanny, I am averse to fair-skinned people while having a special regard for tawnier faces. (114)

The nanny's "dark," "fearsome looks" and "dreadful physique" and the love she inspires in the young Taj al-Saltanah are conceptualized as at odds with each other. The nanny transcends her natural shortcomings in her devotion to her young charge: "Here I find it necessary to describe this woman's physical appearance so that the reader may be acquainted with her, since she was so diligent in the refinement of my character and my upbringing" (114). Taj al-Saltanah's need to dwell on her nanny's appearance reveals that this woman's unpleasant physique remains something to be overcome. This exception to the seemingly organic integration of race, class, and aesthetics is replicated in Taj al-Saltanah's description of her mother: "My mother belonged to the royal family, being a first cousin to my father's. When I was born, she was very young, very beautiful, and very virtuous. Profoundly given to piety and devotion, she spent all her hours praying to God, reading the scripture and reciting from it. . . . But this was not enough: being a good princess does not necessarily translate into being a good mother" (109–110). By way of proof she later demonstrates: "The love between Matron Nanny and me had grown so deep that I shied away from my dearly-revered mother completely. If she tried to hold me in her arms and kiss me, I screamed and ran at once to the refuge of my nanny's arms" (114). She goes on to describe how her adoration for the nanny made her want to imitate even her accent and manner of speech. Finally she turns her attention back to the focus of the initial comparison: "How I wish I could have felt the same tenderness for my venerable mother that I did for my nanny, a tenderness I am trying to describe here! Then I could tell you about her, rather than about an unimportant black woman. But alas, wrong-headed thinking and artificiality conspired with pomposity and unnecessary pandering to turn the childhood sweetness of maternal love into a bitter taste in my mouth, and kept me away from my worshipful mother's arms" (115). Here the force of Taj al-Saltanah's bitterness toward her mother makes her forget her earlier disregard for the dictates of class and race and returns the nanny to social and racial categories appropriate for her. This is not to say that Taj al-Saltanah has lost sight of her love for the nanny, but rather that her chagrin over being deprived of maternal love makes her demote the nanny to "an unimportant black woman." Evoking the sense of abandonment she felt as a child is the true impetus for this sudden imposition of distance: the nanny, in spite of all her affection and care, could not replace the "natural" bond between mother and child. We will have occasion to

return to Taj al-Saltanah's views on the crucial role mothers play in the formation of their children's characters.

On the topic of the nanny, however, Taj al-Saltanah's continues to struggle with her contradictory attitudes. Although she would like to live by her
own maxim, 'the consummate man'[3] does not judge others by outward appearances, but by the accomplishments within" (232), when she turns to describing her brother's entourage, she falls back into observations of this
nature: "Nur al-Dawla, the mother of Salar al-Dawla, on the other hand, was
a tribeswoman from Azerbaijan, quite plebeian and not particularly attractive.
As for Khazen-e Aqdas, she was a negress" (233). It is this woman's family
connection with Taj al-Saltanah's nanny that softens the ensuing description:

> When the telegraph announcing my father's assassination reached the Shah
> and he prepared to leave for Tehran to ascend the throne, he immediately be-
> stowed titles on all his family, young or old. It was at this time that Olfat be-
> came Khazen-e Aqdas (Most Blessed Confidante). Enjoying the king's
> special favor, this lady had his ear and wielded considerable influence. It gave
> me great joy to see my beloved nanny's cousin covered with diamonds and
> crown jewels. As you know, my dear teacher, being an artist yourself, a black
> face is nicely enhanced by white jewelry, particularly if it is shiny. But what
> brought me the greatest inner happiness, my teacher, was the fact that this
> woman had retained her accent; most of her words were identical to my
> nanny's, very funny and sweet. (233)

The internal battle displayed in this passage reveals the convergence of several
conflicting forces. The speed with which her brother, the new king, elevates
his friends and relations into nobility is targeted by Taj al-Saltanah for ridicule.
By outlining the incongruent grouping her brother brought to the royal
court, she emphasizes his being out of his element. It is a mark of her
brother's lack of culture that leads him to elevate Azerbaijani tribeswomen

---

3. The Persian uses a gender-neutral term, *insan*, "a human being."

and "negresses" to the highest ranks in the king's household. But as Taj al-Saltanah is engaged in this description of her brother's ineptitude and lack of social cultivation, she finds herself confronted with the old tenderness she feels for her nanny and her relations. Thus, interwoven into the sarcastic tone in which she speaks of seeing the crown jewels on her nanny's cousin is a half-hearted expression of pleasure at the sight of the "natural" beauty of a black woman bedecked with white jewels. The aside to her teacher and mention of the artistic understanding they share is an attempt both to justify her delight at this socially incongruous vision and to distance herself from the "absurdity" of the scene.

Taj al-Saltanah is both implicated in the values of her class and times and at war with them. She does indeed want to make her nanny and her racial and social subjugation stand in stark contrast to the woman's humanity, dedication, and love, especially as the nanny's marginality sets up links with Taj al-Saltanah's own sense of alienation and loneliness. This affinity for the marginalized of her society is evident elsewhere in her memoirs, for instance in the description of a friendship Taj al-Saltanah strikes up with an Armenian seamstress, Anna, while staying in Azerbaijan.

The introduction to this segment of the memoirs emphasizes Taj al-Saltanah's isolation: "In this land of strangers, my sole companion and friend was an Armenian girl named Anna" (270). The one paragraph devoted to Anna is sandwiched between one revealing Taj al-Saltanah's husband's philandering, which opened up an ever-increasing gap between the couple, and her sense of not being felt welcome at the crown prince's inner sanctum, where she used to make regular visits. Squarely in the middle of this dual familial rejection, Taj al-Saltanah interjects a close bond of friendship with Anna: "She was eighteen years old, pretty, with beautiful dark eyes, and made her living as a seamstress. A month after we arrived, when I needed to have a new dress made, this girl was sent for. Little by little, I became close to her. She bore an equally sincere love for me and was often in my house. In the corners of her large, dark eyes, there were often teardrops that sparkled like diamonds. With a pleasant voice she would say, 'I love you.' Her voice penetrated to the core of my being, and I listened for it with eagerness" (270). In contrast to the nanny whose physical appearance does not match the depth of her emotions, Anna's whole being exudes the harmony Taj al-Saltanah is missing in other realms of her own life. The love and companionship denied to her by her husband and relatives is encapsulated and elevated to a romantic attachment in the figure of the Armenian seamstress.

That the inclusion of this friendship at this stage of the narration is necessitated by the loneliness Taj al-Saltanah experiences during this period of her life is confirmed both by the position it occupies in the narrative and by the exaggerated nature of the description. The tears in Anna's eyes, the declaration of love, and the manner in which these expressions affect Taj al-Saltanah appear unmotivated unless read against this statement in the next paragraph: "I was so caught up in despair and under so much pressure from being among strangers that I had forgotten the world and everything in it" (270). Like the nanny, Anna fills an emotional void. Her minority status, not unlike nanny's racial distinctions, strike up correspondences with Taj al-Saltanah's sense of being surrounded by strangers and her feeling completely isolated. Their being "other" is the point on which Taj al-Saltanah's emotions converge.

This emphasis on the marginalized reappears in other aspects of Taj al-Saltanah's memoirs. For instance, when discussing her mother's faulty method of child rearing, she removes the blame from her mother as an individual and, instead, focuses on the lot of Persian women: "Heaven forbid if it seems that I am disavowing my mother, for whom I hold a devout reverence! No, she was not to blame. But I must reproach the traditions and ethos of a nation that barred the way toward happiness to all women and held them, wretched and unenlightened, in a world of utmost ignorance" (110). She continues her line of thought and concludes that "all moral defects or evils in this country have originated and spread from the absence of education for women" (110). It is such assertions that have led scholars to identify Taj al-Saltanah as an early Persian feminist and an advocate of women's rights. Yet, her "feminism" is also riddled with contradictions. Some of these contradictions can be traced to her conflictual relationship with her mother. A reexamination of the manner and specifics of this relationship might open new vistas on Taj al-Saltanah's views on women's liberation and shed some light on her troubled and tenuous relations with Persian women.

Taj al-Saltanah's first mention of her views on the oppression of Persian women coincides with the presentation of her own birth and genealogy. It is when she introduces her mother that she launches into an analysis of the importance of women's education. She enhances the previously cited argument by adding: "All those that have contributed to the world's history were raised by educated mothers and by fathers who encouraged reform, whereupon they became leaders in industry and invention, and true servants of world civilization. Similarly, great warriors, true liberators, and genuine freedom-lovers have been brought into the world and raised by capable mothers" (110). The terms she uses in this passage appear to echo the language and spirit of the Constitutionalist era and its preoccupation with reform, freedom, and progress. Interestingly, however, Taj al-Saltanah blends into this rhetoric of modernization a historical perspective at odds with it. Although the purported aim of her presentation is to highlight the significance of education for responsible motherhood, she veers into a past hardly coterminous with the vision of modernity implied in terms such as "industry and invention."

For illustrations of her argument Taj al-Saltanah draws on an historical overview reaching back into Greek and Roman civilization: "The people of Sparta, for example, though themselves savage and uncouth, trained their children in the art of warfare so well that they were able to preserve their independence for years and to destroy Athens, the capital of Greece" (110). The fact that Taj al-Saltanah finds it necessary to remark on the savagery and uncouthness of Spartans before proceeding to her discussion of the value they attached to the upbringing of their children as proper warriors indicates that the ground has shifted from under her discourse on the benefits of modern education. The anecdote she relates from the history of Sparta appears to be an illustration of maternal support and encouragement: "on returning from battle a son said to his mother, 'My sword is too short.' She calmly replied, 'My dear, take one step further!' " (110). In this seemingly out-of-place anecdote we find the central thread running through Taj al-Saltanah's analysis of the role of

mothers: the need for unconditional support that she found lacking in her relationship with her mother. That this thread does not necessarily tie into the
discussions of women's education is illustrated by the tortuous way in which
the narrative takes a detour through the absence of maternal love in Taj
al-Saltanah's life to return to the larger problem confronting all Persian
women. In fact, later on, she includes herself among these deficient Persian
mothers.

While pointing out the importance of breast-feeding, she writes:

> Take me, for example. I have four children, all of whom are fully grown. Al-
> though I made every effort to educate all four, each has his own character.
> When I ponder the issue, I see that their characters are replicas of their wet
> nurses'; they certainly do not take after me in any way, and I find that their
> wet nurses live on in them. Had I breast-fed and raised them myself, had that
> natural affection been coupled with maternal love, I never would have aban-
> doned them during their childhood; nor would I have separated from their
> father, albeit I suffered a thousand torments and was afflicted and miserable
> every hour of my life. (115–16)

Breast-feeding becomes emblematic of maternal love. Had she breast-fed her
children, she would have been more successful in instilling in them her own
character traits: " 'Naught but what is in the jug shall ooze from it' " (116).
This image of the child as a vessel into which is poured, along with mother's
milk, maternal love owes much to the reformist discourses of the times. In
"Crafting An Educated Housewife," Afsaneh Najmabadi describes the changing images of maternity in educational treatises written by Persian reformists:
"Not only did the bearer of the womb regulate the character of the fetus, but
now the regulatory process turned back upon womb/woman. National formation began with the womb. If differently constructed Iranians were to be
produced, woman as potential mother needed to be regulated and reconstructed. But the new notion of schooling also heralded new rights: because of
the womb's central importance, 'one needs to pay especial attention to and
care for women and their rights so that children will not become ill-tempered

and bad-natured' " (1998, 93). Taj al-Saltanah's declaration that "obviously, education at home begins before school" (118) underscores women's role in "produc[ing] children worthy of modernity" (Najmabadi 1998, 94). As Najmabadi points out "motherhood became a mediating term between two concepts central to modernity: progress and women's rights," creating "disciplinary and emancipatory moments that enabled each other's work." But, in Zohreh Sullivan's words, these emancipatory impulses were subject to "the simultaneity of modernity and its underside" (1998, 224): "Both modernity and feminism, in Iran and elsewhere, exist in perpetual antithesis with excluded particularities that remain beyond their control, and return to disrupt their management" (216). Taj al-Saltanah's memoirs are one of the sites in which these dialectical tensions play themselves out.

Terms such as motherhood and modernity become ambiguous signs in Taj al-Saltanah's narrative. At times they afford her the possibility of imagining a new gendered national identity, but, at other times, they become barriers to analyzing the full extent of Persia's social problems. For instance, her extensive discussion of the role of mothers is juxtaposed with a curious absolving of fathers. Probably motivated by her admiration for her father, she does not offer a balanced view of equality of the sexes she otherwise advocates. For instance, when discussing her marriage at an early age, she notes with a great deal of passion: "Ah misery! Of mankind's great misfortunes one is this, that one must take a wife or husband according to the wishes of one's parents. This bizarre custom does not stand to reason and is contrary to law. Here the Europeans are right—but then they surpass us in all areas of learning and progress" (150). In a passage immediately preceding this one, she writes of her own husband: "This lifelong mate of mine I had accepted in theory, nurturing in my imagination merely the idea of husband and wholly oblivious of a husband's sweeping prerogatives" (149–150). This critique of the all-embracing powers given a Persian husband would suggest that, when discussing matters not pertaining to her father, she is more than willing to address the inequality of the sexes in Persian marriages and families. But her progressive views are always sidetracked by her concern for her father's image. In fact, she marshals all the knowledge she has accumulated through her readings into the service of anchoring her character flaws solely in the absence of maternal love. She ends her whirlwind summary of world history with this: "It is the mother, then, that first opens the door to happiness for her children. Unfortunately, this pathway to well-being was closed to me, and it is here that the great misfortunes of my subsequent life found their source" (112).

The fact that she felt bereft of maternal love left an indelible mark on her character. We see the renewed anguish in her retelling of how, as a child, she reacted to the birth of a brother on whom all of her mother's affection were focused:

[O]wing to the strange predictions and particular aspirations of the time, the boy received preferential treatment. This was supposed to be a subtle form of preference, not an obvious one. But I was so intelligent and alert that they could not hide anything from me. Sensing this partiality on my mother's part, I felt slighted and became more withdrawn from her. Sometimes I felt so unhappy that I considered myself the most unfortunate human being. From that time I began to develop a great hardness of heart, setting off on my journey through life with a condition akin to lunacy. (140)

In this description, as in the introduction to her childhood, Taj al-Saltanah embarks on an exploration of the causes of her unhappiness. Her "education" in European letters, history, and sciences has convinced her that everything is subject to causal laws of nature. Armed with her newly acquired knowledge, she sets out to test this theory in her own life. True to her "naturalist" beliefs, she begins with the premise, resembling Rousseau's, that all human beings are created happy and equal and it is society that corrupts that original state of bliss and equality.

We see reflections of this belief in the inherent equality of human beings in her statements about the plight of servants. Her observation of the treatment of the servants leads her to write: "This grieved me tremendously and left me heart-sick, and I would ask myself, 'What difference is there between them and the ladies, except that the latter wear satin dresses and God has chosen to favor them with worldly belongings? So why should the former be the dominated, and the latter the dominators?' " (160). On the level of abstractions, she finds herself drawn to the notions of liberty and equality. When these precepts are imported into her personal life, they often clash with others already in place. She embraces wholeheartedly a reorganization of family structures that would release women from their subservience, educate them, thereby enabling them to raise more responsible members of society. Her distance from her mother, however, makes this plan much more amenable to a redefinition of the role of mothers. Her father, whose love for her she believes to have been unconditional, she cannot include in this revision. As a result, the burden for the success of social reform falls squarely on mothers' shoulders.

The stress I have placed on the direct link between Taj al-Saltanah's views on women's, and more specifically mothers', education and her troubled relationship with her own mother is not intended to distort her image as a progressive woman.[4] Instead, I want to demonstrate how much her readings of that which happened outside Persia were incorporated into her own experiences and were modified to fit the conflictual patterns of her life history.

The peculiar twists Taj al-Saltanah gives her readings of new ideas on motherhood are not the only manifestations of her self-referentiality. Even the notion of the inherent equality of all human beings gets deflected from the larger social scale to her personal dilemmas: "I looked upon my childhood captivity with an analytical sense of regret, thinking to myself, 'Why should man,[5] who has been created to live free, be slave to the wishes of others and live his life according to their behest? There are no distinctions among people; all are alike. All can live in natural freedom' " (160). If Taj al-Saltanah makes no distinction between her own "captivity" and the numerous other types of enslavement she would have had occasion to observe, it is a measure of the anguish she suffered as a child and adolescent. By creating a fellowship with all

4. For an analysis of Taj al-Saltanah's participation in the progressive movements of the time, see Janet Afary's *The Iranian Constitutional Revolution 1906–1911: Grassroots Democracy, Social Democracy, and the Origins of Feminism* (1996, 177–208).

5. On the translation of "man" see note 3 above.

others who have been deprived of freedom, she succeeds in forming a community, albeit tenuous and imaginary, for herself.

While here she is an enthusiastic believer in the inherent equality of all human beings, elsewhere she insists on setting herself apart from, and above, others. On the level of character and appearance, for instance, her self-description dwells on her exceptional traits:

> First of all, I must describe my appearance and character as a child. I was exceptionally intelligent and clever; it seemed that God had spread open the wings of his bounty over me. I had beautiful brown hair, long and naturally curly. My complexion was rosy, my eyes dark, and my eyelashes long. The picture was completed by a well-proportioned nose, small mouth and lips, and white teeth that gave a wonderful glow to my ruby lips. In the royal palace, which was the gathering spot for the choicest of lovely women, there was no face prettier or lovelier than mine. Truly, I was a beautiful, adorable child. (119)

Taj al-Saltanah's inability to see anything but perfection in herself contradicts her assertion that no one should be judged by appearances. This flawless self-portrait also belies the inner turmoils she traces to the earliest stages of her childhood. As I have demonstrated before, the emphasis on appearance has to be understood in the context of two conflicting sets of values: one that commodifies women and ranks them according to their beauty and a more modern standard based on the value of women's education and independence of spirit. That Taj al-Saltanah cannot resolve the tension between these two opposites is manifested in her writing about women's suffrage.

When addressing the rights of women in general, she includes herself in a community of "Persian women . . . set aside from humankind" (284) whose condition she contrasts with that of their European and American counterparts:

> How I wish I could travel to Europe and meet these freedom-seeking ladies! I would say to them, "As you fight for your rights happily and honorably, and

emerge victorious in your aims, do cast a look at the continent of Asia. Look into the houses, where the walls are three or five meters high and the only entryway is a door guarded by a doorman. Beneath the chains of captivity and resistless weight of subjugation you will see a mass of oppressed cripples, some sallow and pale-faced, others bare and hungry, yet others endlessly expectant and mournful." I would add, "these are women too; these are human, too. These are also worthy of due respect and merit. See how life treats them." (285)

The passion and conviction of Taj al-Saltanah's statements lose none of their intensity in the ensuing passages in which she relates the answers she provided to a questionnaire sent by an Armenian "freedom fighter for Persia" to several Persian women of high birth. In point form, she continues to argue that the success of any social reform in Persia is contingent on the inclusion of women in all levels of life. Unveiling women, for instance, she points out at the end of her response, would increase the nation's productivity: "Now if these two-thirds [women] were employed in meaningful work, the nation would make two-fold progress, and everyone would be wealthy" (290).

The social consciousness and the sense of camaraderie and practicality we see in this part of Taj al-Saltanah's text is severely undercut in the last pages of the fragment. Describing her increasing alienation from her husband and family, she turns her anger on the very women whose rights she has just defended so eloquently:

All the women of Persia, whether high or low, related to me or not, were my enemies because of my good looks. Their enmity was heightened when they saw that my looks were complemented by a pleasant disposition, kindness, and good nature. I had a great desire for learning and took every opportunity I could to improve my understanding. On this front, too, I was ahead of the other ladies in conversation, demeanor, and general knowledge, and this was one more reason for their jealousy. They saw that I was accomplished in all respects. All my life I have had to put up with a general envy. These people made my life so difficult, and inflicted such harm, that no human has suffered as I have. But I never lost my composure. God was always with me and protected me from mischief and venom of all that hostility. (302–3)

Taj al-Saltanah's vehemence bears witness to her inner conflicts and her desire to integrate the aesthetics of female beauty and the dictates of a modern gendered identity.

There were many factors that reinforced Taj al-Saltanah's distrust of her community. She felt betrayed by her husband, whose philandering was a constant source of embarrassment to her. She alludes to an abortion she decided upon when she discovered that her husband had contracted gonorrhea. It appears that she never fully recovered from the medication she took to induce this abortion: "For three years I was unwell and nervous. The illness had changed me completely; my attitudes and behavior were different. I was capricious, quick-tempered and irascible. No longer able to cope with the slightest annoyance, I would quickly lose my composure and become indisposed and bed-ridden in misery. . . . For a while, by virtue of the malady of 'hysteria,' I obtained some relief from confinement to the house" (301). It is worth noting that some of the terms she uses to describe her changed temperament are similar to her childhood character traits, or at least ones she associates with her childhood. In other words, in moments of personal crisis, she sees herself as completely alienated from her fellow human beings. It is at such times that she falls back on her childlike self-glorification. As if to confirm the validity of the label of a hysteric, a term she clearly adopts uncritically, she loses her earlier analytical calm and begins to enumerate the ways in which she stands apart from all other Persian women: "Among all the women of Persia there was none so pretty as I. Whenever I attended large gatherings—weddings, feasts, royal audiences, and other formal occasions—at which there were almost a thousand princesses and women of high birth, I was always the most beautiful" (302). This is reminiscent of an earlier passage, from the night of her wedding, when she finds herself ignored by the young bridegroom: "There was a large mirror in this room in which I could see the whole length of my body. I found myself incredibly pretty, like a queen or goddess. I wondered in surprise why my husband did not kneel and worship me" (241).

Taj al-Saltanah's retreats into such apparent narcissism both as a child and as an adult refocus our vision of her anxieties about herself and her place in a changing society. In one sense, she wants to return, like Rousseau's solitary walker, to the brooding solitude with which she opens her memoirs. Like the solitary walker, she does find herself alone in the world, deprived of all human understanding and companionship. In another sense, she embraces the changes taking place around her, adapts herself to the new model of progress and education, and longs for reintegration into society.

This perpetual intertwining of gravitation toward solitude and human companionship is best illustrated in the scene of her first courtship by the same young man who had regretted his decision to marry Taj al-Saltanah's sister. The scene she recalls dates back to an evening when she finds herself alone with one of her father's wives. The two women set out on a walk on the palace grounds, and this is how Taj al-Saltanah describes her impressions of that promenade:

> We were both young, I almost a child and she almost an adolescent. In the still silence of the night we walked firmly and quietly on the gravel. Looking at the moon, which shone with a strange glow, each was busy with her own thoughts. Calm and stillness had enveloped the promenade, and the air was so barren of sound that it echoed with our slightest movement, our quietest sound. The reigning silence produced an effect as of nature having gone to sleep and laying its head on the pillow of death's brother. Joining hands with this silence was the darkness of the night, which added to one's fears. The eardrum, straining in every direction, despaired of vibrating with any sound. Only the tree branches waving in the evening breeze punctured the silence with their echo. (163–64)

In many ways, this scene is reminiscent of the opening passage of the memoirs. Here again Taj al-Saltanah is not alone, but is lost in her thoughts, and her senses register only silence and stillness. In contrast to the earlier passage, however, her pensiveness is given a far more specific designation. Both in the segment I have quoted and in the paragraph that follows it, fear is mentioned: "The gentle light of the moon, piercing the leaves to fall upon the ground, inspired a sense of fear" (164). There are many levels on which this fear can be interpreted. There is the child's fear of darkness and the absolute stillness of the night. Moreover, Taj al-Saltanah and her companion have wandered a good distance away from others who are congregated for dinner and entertainment. In other words, they have left behind the familiar environment and abandoned themselves to nature, which proves to be a source of both excitement and foreboding.

This immersion in the forces of nature anticipates the arousal of Taj al-Saltanah's passions. When she hears "a stifled sound from the middle of the trees," she pleads with her companion to return to the living quarters. It is at this point that she finds out that the object of the walk was to discover whether she reciprocates the young man's love. Taj al-Saltanah's response to her suitor's messenger is, on the surface, well within the moral bounds: " 'Please tell him from me that I do not consent to this and you are forbidden to raise the subject' " (169). With this, she turns back to the palace.

The description of this retracing of steps is emblematic of Taj al-Saltanah being caught between what she perceives as "natural" and social forces. While walking back, she first notices the beauty of the natural surroundings: "A total silence, reminiscent of the silence of death, surrounded us. We were each thinking our own thoughts, walking toward the garden path very slowly. All around us, flowers and blossoms were filling the air with fragrance, and a soft, cool breeze touched my mournful burning cheeks" (169). Unlike the earlier scene in which she was engulfed in a sense of foreboding, here the narrator finds nature a source of peace and harmony. Yet, the earlier menacing aspect of nature returns, as she contemplates the love the young man has expressed for her: "I found myself standing at the edge of a bottomless precipice whose opening had been covered up with variegated, colorful flowers; the slightest slip, and I would be sucked in" (169). This implies that Taj al-Saltanah sees love and passion as natural phenomena, but ones that she, in her position, cannot openly embrace.

Later that same evening, the young man approaches her and delivers to her flowers in which "was a little card with only the words, 'I love you' " (173). The way in which Taj al-Saltanah records her reaction to this note is an interesting illustration of her dilemma: "This was the second time that night that I was hearing the word 'love' from someone other than my mother or father. It seemed as strange and repulsive in my sight as did the guillotine to the condemned." Taj al-Saltanah's view of herself as a victim has to be understood in the context of her youth. Even in this light, her quandary is to negotiate a path between nature and society, or, as we have seen in her critique of her society, to make the social imitate what she perceives as the inherently salutary natural order. For instance, she lays the foundation of a better Persian society on closer ties between mothers and their offspring. Because she loves her father "naturally" and unconditionally, she cannot fault any aspect of his character, as monarch or father.

The dichotomy she sets up between nature and society proves difficult to maintain, particularly in her self-portrayal. Attempting to place herself on the side of nature, she is nevertheless drawn to the very society she critiques and shuns. Even as a solitary walker, she is comforted by the knowledge that she can turn back to the company of others. Similarly, while she longs to travel to Europe, her imagination is deeply caught within the borders of Persia. She wants to reach out to European and American suffragists, but she also wants to be the most beautiful among Persian women.

Like many Persians of her generation, Taj al-Saltanah embraced the language and spirit of reform. In her analysis of Persian government and society, for instance, she claims to "be guided by nothing except my Persianness and my conscience" (267). As in other facets of Taj al-Saltanah's text, this Persianness is imbued with paradoxes. This same sense of national loyalty inspires her to embrace democracy, progress, and education, but it cannot be allowed to contaminate the image of her father as a just and compassionate ruler. She even falsely attributes the granting of the Persian Constitution to her father.

The distortions and paradoxes of Taj al-Saltanah's memoirs are perpetual reminders to us of the strife between what she herself calls her properly socialized self and the mercurial, second self. If she found any resolution to this

perennial inner conflict, it was in the composition of her life history. By writing about her feelings of being abandoned by her mother and later shunned
by her husband, Taj al-Saltanah was able to put together a portrait of herself
that identified the sources of her loneliness as a child and estrangement as an
adult. In this process, she came face to face with a child who missed maternal
love and was terrified of losing her father's protection. But the adult narrator
could also take comfort in the knowledge that the child's distress could have
been averted through better methods of child rearing. She could also find the
roots of her failed marriage in Persian women's limited education and their
utter seclusion from public life.

The success of Taj al-Saltanah's autobiographical venture, insofar as it
gave her an understanding of herself, allowed her to balance the didactic elements of Persian biography with more subjective strains of self-exploration.
This innovative aspect of Taj al-Saltanah's project should not be underesti-
mated. Unlike the Persians who undertook physical journeys away from their
home and their familiar surroundings, Taj al-Saltanah did not have the luxury
of defining herself against an external other. For her, this other, although
shaped by her readings in European history and literature, was very much part
of the self. The absence of physical journey made for a metaphorical voyage
around the self that turned up many more challenges than Persian travelers
had encountered in the course of actual journeys.

The lack of closure, reflected in both the extant manuscript of Taj
al-Saltanah's life history and the absence of a unified voice and subject, points
up the dilemma of speaking as a woman in a moment of Persian history that
elevates women to new positions of authority and responsibility and at the
same time requires that women perform their new functions within delimited
spheres. In her own account of enlightened women, Taj al-Saltanah emphasizes the need for their self-sacrifice in the creation of a modern nation. But
she also excludes herself from the rank of devoted mothers who brought up
children worthy of the nation. The contradictions she could not resolve in her
life have continued to haunt the national imagination. In a postscript to the
English translation of her memoirs, we read: "Taj saw herself . . . as a liberated
socialite whose life mirrored her commitment to women's emancipation. The

comparison she reportedly made between herself and the famous nineteenth-century French novelist, George Sand, was not far-fetched" (313). The problems of self-representation that required George Sand to pass as a man in the French social and literary circles of her time also emerge in Taj al-Saltanah's desire to dress for a new ideal of Persian womanhood. By unveiling herself, however, Taj al-Saltanah merely reveals the blind spots in Persian views of the liberated, but beautiful, self-sacrificing, and chaste woman. The staying power of these paradoxes is manifest in the last paragraph of the postscript: "Taj's later years must have been fraught with hardship. She died in Tehran in February 1963, an obese and impoverished woman." This testimonial of the social and physical losses suffered by Taj al-Saltanah acts as an invitation to explore what we continue to keep missing in our constructions of Persian female identity.

5

A Performer Manqué

The complex negotiations of gender and national identity manifested in Taj al-Saltanah's memoirs are also reflected in Najmeh Najafi's and Helen Hinckley's *Persia Is My Heart*. But different constraints enter into Najafi's performance of identity. Her text, written in English, addresses an American audience for whose benefit certain models of Persianness are adapted. In conformity with the new placement of women at the core of the formation of the nation, Najafi's self-representation moves to capture the heart of the nation. But her representation of the nation must also be transplanted onto an American stage. The demands for stageworthiness of this text and its consumability by an American audience are attested to in the status it gained among a generation of Peace Corps volunteers who were given *Persia Is My Heart* as an introduction to the country they were about to visit.[1] The need to represent Persia to Americans is steeped in the history of this particular moment in the relations between the two nations.

Persia Is My Heart was published in New York in 1953. The year is ripe with significance: it recalls the nationalization of the oil industry in Persia, accompanied with the spread of nationalist fervor, the American-led coup that

---

1. When I selected Najafi's text for my analysis I was not aware of this fact. I gave a presentation on *Persia Is My Heart* at the Second Biennial Conference on Iranian Studies in May 1998 in Bethesda, after which Bill Hanaway and others told me how they had come across this text. I am grateful to my Persianist colleagues for this information. I owe a special debt of gratitude to the late Latifeh Yarshater for sharing with me memories of her encounters with Najmeh Najafi.

restored Mohammad Reza Shah Pahlavi to power, and the beginning of a new, problematic era in Persian-American relations. Najmeh Najafi's narrative is written against this background and is direct in addressing the fears of potential American investors. Persia's readiness for American-style capitalism and her eagerness to embrace social and political reform are subtexts in this attempt to illustrate a model for mutually beneficial interactions between Persians and Americans.

The American government had already invested resources in orchestrating a coup against what they perceived to be an increasing convergence of communist and nationalist sentiments. In Roy Mottahedeh's account of the coup we see the beginnings of an investment of American capital in Persia:

> The coup succeeded with a speed that surprised its supporters almost as much as its opponents. It was largely organized by Teddy Roosevelt's grandson Kermit Roosevelt, according to Kermit's account. . . . On August 18, 1953, the Iranian army, angry that the demonstrations mounted by the Iranian communists seemed to imply that with the Shah's departure the Communists were calling the tune, put down these demonstrations with a heavy hand and with loud expressions of support for the Shah. On the morning of August 19 a crowd, bought in southern Tehran for only $100,000 by Roosevelt's men—a crowd that included professional bazaar toughs, prostitutes, some religious leaders, and even some sincere secular royalists—marched toward the center of the city and attacked [the prime minister's] office. . . . Suddenly there were signs of pro-American and pro-Shah sentiment everywhere, and Kermit Roosevelt still had $900,000 funds in a safe. A few days later the Americans announced a grant of $45 million to the Iranian government and promised further aid. (1985, 130)

I dwell on this historical moment to shed light on the workings of power and capital in the idea of the nation Najafi is at pains to embody. The feminization and infantalization of the Persia she nestles in her heart are mirrored in her self-representations. Interestingly these very images are picked up by the Iranian writer and activist Jalal Al-e Ahmad in his 1961 treatise, *Plagued by the*

West. Describing the ills besetting Persia in his coinage "westitis," he writes: "The west-stricken man is a gigolo. He is effeminate. He is always primping; always making sure of his appearance. He has even been known to pluck his eyebrows! He places great importance on his shoes, his clothes, and his home" (1982, 70). Al-e Ahmad's critique of the imperialist and capitalist ventures in Persia intersects with Najafi's representation in the gendering of the nation, highlighting the persistence of the very paradoxes of modernity we witnessed in Taj al-Saltanah's memoirs. In sharp contrast to Al-e Ahmad, Najafi advocates a model of collaboration between Persia and the West, ultimately riddled with its own inner contradictions.

1953 has its echoes on the title page of *Persia Is My Heart*, which announces: *"Persia Is My Heart* told by Najmeh Najafi to Helen Hinckley." The relationship between the American and the Persian woman is left vague. Copyright is attributed to both, but the extent of Helen Hinckley's, or Helen Hinckley Jones as announced on the copyright page, contribution is not mentioned. That the collaboration between the two women was long-lasting is borne out in the subsequent publication of *Reveille for a Persian Village* (1958) and *A Wall and Three Willows* (1967).

It is only in their last coauthored work that additional information is revealed about both writers. After a brief sketch of Najafi's life, it is indicated that while attending Pasadena City College, she met Helen Hinckley, whose own remarks are then cited: "When Najmeh Najafi was a student she lived as a 'borrowed daughter' in our home. I became interested in Najmeh and her dream, and because her English was limited, I helped her write her first book, *Persia Is My Heart*" (1967, 213). In Hinckley's adoption of Najafi as her "borrowed daughter" there is an interesting echo of the American paternal enfolding of Persia in its grasp.

The only other information we are given about Helen Hinckley suggests that she might have acted as Najafi's ghostwriter. At the end of the same note about the authors in *A Wall and Three Willows*, we read: "In addition to her own writing Helen Hinckley has taught a course in Writing for Publication at Pasadena City College for twenty years."

As Najmeh Najafi's ghostwriter, Helen Hinckley disappears into the background. The subtleness of this presence and involvement is a far cry from the manner in which Persian history was being shaped by American players. The narrative voice in *Persia Is My Heart* is firmly linked to the Persian, and there are no obvious slips of the kind made by Remón, the Spanish cowriter of the *Don Juan of Persia*. Unlike Remón, Hinckley is not even given the role of Najafi's translator. In fact, the text has a rough linguistic texture, reinforcing the impression that Najafi's English is indeed "limited." On the surface at least, Hinckley's role is to observe the drama of identity Najmeh Najafi stages.

It is this staging to which I wish to turn in this chapter. Focusing primarily on *Persia Is My Heart*, with occasional attention to the two later works produced by Najafi and Hinckley, I will explore the construction of Najafi's identity at different cultural crossroads. The stress I place on *Persia Is My Heart* stems from this work's own deliberate assembling of the protagonist's past in Persia and its retracing of her steps from Persia to the United States. Interestingly, Najafi's journey itself is never described; the scenes depicted for us are either set in Persia or in the United States. We know Najafi as a young woman living in Persia, or as a student in an American university. This intriguing suspension of the moment of crossing in *Persia Is My Heart* seems to signal a need to rush through the difficult in-between state. I will later examine representations of Najafi's return journey home in *Reveille for a Persian Village*, but first I will turn my attention to the narrative strategies of the first work in an attempt to grasp the way in which her identity is made to fit the image of Persia as an anxious and grateful recipient of American aid and protection. At times Najafi's gendered self-articulation becomes inseparable from the representation of her nation as an exotic and coy object to be desired and pursued.

A blanket of exoticism envelops the form and the content of the narrative. As I have already noted, *Persia Is My Heart* is presented as a tale told by a Persian to an American. Apart from the illusion of spontaneity, this conceit invokes an old tradition of storytelling whose continuity Najafi emphasizes in her own family. Addressing the effect stories have had on her imagination, the narrator places herself in an unbroken heritage that relegates Persia to timelessness. Najafi tells us that her mother's cousin, whose thinness prompted Najafi to secretly call her the Match, as in a matchstick, played an important role in instilling a love of stories in her: "Her gift of words. That was the gift I wanted. When I was four or five I used to return from seeing a moving picture with Mosen and my older brother, Jafa, would pay me ten cents, even twenty cents for retelling the story to him. I liked the feeling of importance that his listening gave me. Someday, I hoped, people would listen to me and live in my words as we did in the words of The Match" (31). Najafi's craving for an audience might well explain why *Persia Is My Heart* is billed as a story she tells an American friend. As Najafi reveals in the same segment of her book, the other aspect of storytelling she learned from the Match was the need to tailor a story to the tastes of her audience. She remembers her horror at hearing an abrupt and violent ending the Match gave one of her stories. Equally well preserved in her memory is the speed with which the Match changed the ending with a simple "No, I was wrong" (31) in order to please her audience. This early lesson in storytelling gives Najafi the awareness of the need for both an attentive audience and a storyteller's sensitivity to that audience's expectations. She draws on these skills in *Persia Is My Heart*.

The book's drawings, or what the title page calls "decorations by Najmeh," who we later find out has a flare for fashion design and sewing, reinforce the storybook quality. "The wedding," "The bathhouse," and "The Mektab" (traditional school) are intended to help the reader visualize the scenes described. Others combine the visual with captions that become fragmentary stories in their own right. "Just a little something made by hand" is written underneath a drawing of a vase, a picture frame, and a small bowl. "A dancing girl. Not too nice, perhaps" and "Ishmael with his magnificent bread" are other captions complementing the seemingly inaccessible Persian art and culture.

The simplicity, to say nothing of the roughness, of these sketches, along with the hints embedded in these captions, serve to return the focus to Najmeh, the storyteller whose own childlike qualities are captured both in the drawings and in the clumsy captions. For instance, the caption accompanying the figure of the dancing girl gives us a glimpse of the position of women in Persian social structures, a topic to which Najafi returns on several occasions. To be a dancing girl is to accept a questionable reputation, hence Najafi's "not too nice, perhaps." The hesitation, signaled in the afterthought, "perhaps," hints at Najafi's opposition, albeit subtle, to the cultural injunction that relegates female performers to an underclass. But this caption does not become an occasion for Najafi to address the status of women in Persian society. Her ambivalence can be better understood in light of an episode she relates from her school days.

At a benefit for victims of a natural disaster, held at Najafi's school, she takes part in a performance. Najafi's role consists of singing the verses of a famous poem by the Persian poet Sa'di. She is accompanied by a chorus of other schoolgirls who later join her in a dance on the stage. It is Najafi's memory of that instance of fame on the stage that echoes back to her sketch of the dancing girl: "After the song we all danced. I felt a special light on me bringing out the whiteness of my robe. If my life were different I would like to sing and dance forever, but this I can never do. Never can I dance or sing for money for myself. There was happiness in the audience because of our singing and dancing, and it flowed toward the stage like a great ocean and engulfed us" (117). The sheer delight young Najmeh experiences on stage is reminiscent of her craving for an audience. She craves performance, be it as a storyteller, singer, or dancer. The repeated "never" in the passage I have just quoted does seem to close the door to any hope of becoming a performer. The incompatibility of personal desires and social strictures produces a tension that cannot be resolved through recourse to the rhetoric of progress and modernity. Therefore the caption accompanying the figure of the dancing girl is left as an uncanny reminder of the same cultural legacy that found expression in Mu'in al-Saltanah's representation of the Persian dancing girls at the Chicago Exposition. If in this instance Najafi cannot challenge this specific example of the cultural encoding of gender without becoming an outlaw, she finds other occasions to give voice to an unequivocal critique of women's status.

The most direct expressions of Najafi's opposition to traditions of female socialization appear in the chapter entitled "Time for Suitors": "There is one half of humanity in my country, however, that has no right to vote, no right to hold office, that until eighteen years ago was considered unworthy even to associate with men outside the home. . . . Women in Persia, as in most other Islamic countries, are a race apart, an inferior, limited race" (81). Echoing Taj al-Saltanah's views on gender relations, Najafi also embraces the demands of modernity. She pursues an education, opens a business as a seamstress, and finally leaves her country for the United States in search of further education and self-fulfillment. The repeated emphasis on herself reinforces the exemplariness of her own trajectory.

In fact, *Persia Is My Heart* is a skillfully staged performance at whose center she places herself and her experiments with identity. This is already signaled in the table of contents with chapter headings like: "My Country," "Myself," "My Letters," "I Know Hunger," "I See History Made," and "I Find My Mind." Yet, she carefully dances around the prominent role she gives her own subjectivity in the structuring of this cross-section of autobiography, social history, and commentary.

For all the emphasis on the first-person personal and possessive pronouns, Najafi does not embark on a confessional life history. Like her decorative sketches, the story of her own past is there only in rough outlines. Of her family history, we glean a few details in passing. Because her father died when she was very young, understandably she has few memories of him. Yet, she acknowledges a lack of curiosity about other aspects of her family history that sometimes she herself finds striking: "My mother had traveled, my father had been many places. I do not know why I didn't beg my mother to tell me of her childhood in Czarist Russia where her father represented Persia; or my father's student days in Egypt and France and Turkey; and of his travels throughout Europe and the Middle East with Ahmad Shah. It simply never occurred to me. Perhaps because in our home those years were in a locked box" (45). She does little to wrench open the locked box in which we would find the answer to questions about her family. Yet, this reluctance to overcome the gaps in her family history is counterbalanced by a delight she takes in sudden revelations that defy the collective reticence in which she appears to be almost unconsciously participating.

That she can speak Turkish, for instance, is a detail we stumble on while she recounts a visit to a village in Azerbaijan. Interestingly, the surprise is shared by Najafi, who even in the retelling of the episode acknowledges her slow and unexpected discovery about herself: "We went at once to the home of the headman. He was a pleasant man whose thin lips seemed carved to a smile and whose black eyes were lively and talkative. He spoke to us in Persian, so far removed from Farsi that it seemed almost a foreign language. Yet I understood him. Suddenly I realized that his Persian was more nearly Turkish than Farsi and I replied in my little Turkish. As soon as I spoke his smile grew wider and his eyes softer and warmer, though still keen and lively"(144). Najafi finds herself at a crossroads between familiarity and foreignness and it is the slow recognition of this alterity within that slips her into the right language for this exchange. Her switching from "Persian" to "Farsi" is an interesting reflection of the momentary psychological slip. The word "Persian" is addressed to her American readers, but as she thinks over the "discovery" of her knowledge of Turkish, she forgets her audience and inserts the word "Farsi," the designation Persians use for their language. The mere articulation of the cross-linguistic encounter in the Azerbaijani village requires her to shift her linguistic allegiances. When she refers to her mother tongue as Farsi, she is signaling her position as an insider, but her familiarity with Turkish distances her enough from "Farsi" to remind her that non-native speakers refer to it as "Persian." Not only does Najafi not explore her psychological reaction to this scene, she does not even explain how she acquired her "little Turkish."

This episode and its narration highlight the constant interplay of discretion with regard to her family, on the one hand, and self-discoveries that require a stepping away from self-concealment. The tension is visible throughout Najafi's narrative, but, far from shutting us out, it draws us into the inner workings of Najafi's staging of identity. Ultimately, the encounter with the village headman is about both Najafi's distant relationship with Turkish, and by extension her genealogy, and the development of her character as a budding social activist.

The narrative moves quickly away from the internal play of self and other into a discussion of the "serious" socioeconomic problems that separate the villagers from the Tehrani visitors on a ski outing: "After the others had gone to ski I made friends with some of the children playing on the stiff crust of the snow. I noticed that their stomachs were distended like those of the children at the train stops. . . . From them I found out that of every three homes in the village only one had enough bread" (144–45). The economic gap between the village and the city alerts Najafi to problems with which she appears to become preoccupied: "At home in Tehran between my visits to the villages I thought of the farmers, of their hopelessness and helplessness. They are patient, frugal, hardworking. Yet theirs is the existence of animals" (157).

Najafi's concern with the level of poverty in her country becomes a central theme and prompts her to provide a sketch of Persia's political history. Interestingly, while even as a child and a teenager she is endowed with keen insight, in her discussions of political events of her own lifetime she seems to be robbed of her astute powers of observation. For instance, in a chapter entitled "I See History Made," she describes her first visit at the age of sixteen to the Persian parliament, the Majlis. She provides a brief outline of the turmoils the country is undergoing at the time she visits the Majlis:

> At Yalta, when the second front was planned, Persia had been promised that six months after the end of hostilities Russia and America and Great Britain would leave our country. According to that promise the United States and Great Britain withdrew but Russia stayed on. Even with Russia worn out from war, Persia could be no match for so great an expanse of land, so great a population, so great a fervor as the political philosophy of the people generated, so great a dictator as conducted the affairs of Russia.
>
> Our one chance was to put the whole matter before the Security Council of the United Nations. (Strong nations like America do not realize what such a Council means to smaller nations.) To prepare for this move the Senate was to hold its first meeting. (169–70)

This depiction of the threat posed by the Soviet Union to Persia's sovereignty reveals much about the sentiments underwriting the collaborations between Najafi and Hinckley. The choice of adjectives in this passage constructs an interesting dynamics of power: the adjective that is found appropriate for describing Russia is great, while Persia is labeled a small nation, and the United States a strong nation. The smallness of Persia vis-à-vis the super powers, established in this earlier part, manifests itself at a later segment of the same chapter.

When it comes to the description of the parliamentary proceedings themselves, Najafi assumes an uncharacteristic innocence and incomprehension: "How can I tell you of the meeting of the Senate? . . . There in the beautiful room the men, rising, quarreled like little children. They spat rude words at each other—words I scarcely knew in Persian and for which I have no English" (173–74). Although depicted from the perspective of an innocent young woman, the scene nevertheless succeeds in reducing and undermining the Persian political figures. Leaving the ineffective and childlike statesmen of Persia behind, the young Najafi immediately embarks on a study of history whose fruits she shares with her readers in an overview of the history of Persian Empire.

Her whirlwind résumé ends with: "Much of modern Persia's history was in my memory. . . . At sixteen I felt that a new period was opening for my country" (186). This signals not merely a learning of Persian history, but rather its internalization in Najafi's own memory and psyche. The possessiveness of this articulation is reflected in the fact that this detour through Persia's history brings us back to the drama at the core of the narrative: the emergence of Najmeh Najafi's social and historical consciousness and her perception of the need to graft herself onto a new model that entails a complete overhaul of her appearance.

Najafi's move toward the adoption of a new wardrobe and its accompanying cultural significance is already signaled in the book's opening passage: "Sitting in the college library bent over my book, *Constitutional History of the United States,* I look like any American school girl. Perhaps I am shorter and more slight than most Western girls, but my clothes are right for America— bobby socks, slim red skirt, white sweater. I turn the pages slowly, slowly. It is not that I find the history uninteresting; my eyes, accustomed to passing from right to left over very different characters, falter, turn back, crawl on again" (1). We are once again confronted with Najafi's appearance concealing and revealing many layers. There is every attempt made to give us a smooth first glance of this Persian out of her element. Her physical appearance, its natural limitations notwithstanding, is carefully calibrated to the American setting without completely erasing the marks of difference that compete with all that is "right for America." But the artificiality and the precariousness of the self-presentation is also brought out in the "faltering" of her eyes in her effort to read a book in English.

This scene is also reminiscent of the passage in *Don Juan of Persia* in which we see the protagonist "constraining" his hand to transcribe Spanish prayers in the Persian alphabet. Striking in both instances is the corporeal reluctance to write and read oneself over into another language. Despite their appearances, the narrators convey a deep-rooted psychological resistance to cultural makeover they go to great lengths to embrace.

The balance the narrator of *Persia Is My Heart* aims for is hinted at in the final passage of the introduction, a seemingly effortless shuttling between languages and cultures: "Sitting in the college library with *Constitutional History of the United States* before me, I think of everything which I am reading in relation to the needs and problems of my own country. I am, at present, an American schoolgirl. But even in America, Persia is my heart" (11). The construct Najafi the cultural cross-dresser creates insists on an inner Persian self, disguised as she might be, devoted to transforming her society and redressing its imbalances. As Yeğenoğlu demonstrates, this logic is at work in many Third World discourses of nationalism that adopt modernity, but distinguish between spiritual and material culture:

In supplying an ideological principle of selection, the nationalist paradigm in fact utilizes the distinction between the material and the spiritual. It is through the mapping of this opposition onto the distinction between outside and inside that the woman's question is articulated to nationalist discourse. . . . This implies that the incorporation of Western principles of rationality and technological development need to be limited to the material world; the spiritual essence of culture must remain uncontaminated by the West, otherwise the features that make the East superior and distinct from the West would disappear and self-identity of the nation would be threatened. (1998, 124)

The protection of the cultural essence falls on the shoulders of women made to fit a new definition "which was not only contrasted with modern Western society, but also distinguished from the indigenous patriarchal tradition" (Yeğenoğlu 1998, 125). Najafi's role as guardian and reformer of her culture conforms with this logic.

Cultural identity, as posited by Najafi, requires a conscious maintenance of distinctions and boundaries. If she appoints herself as a negotiator between Persia and the United States, it is with the design to gain financial support from American investors. She has little need for any cultural baggage that might accompany the financial investments. We develop a better sense of Najafi's design, and its inherent contradictions, in the later stages of her narrative.

The scheme Najafi is trying to promote is in the end a simple one: to convince Americans that investing in Persia is not as risky as they might have assumed after the nationalization of oil. Her earlier discussions of poverty in her homeland and the suffering of the peasants she witnesses firsthand are preludes to what she believes her American audience will require in order to be courted to Persia. They are the kinds of frame stories she, in her wisdom as a storyteller, has deemed appropriate for her audience.

In the final chapter, "The Decision," Najafi drops all pretenses and directly engages with official American policies of the time. Against the backdrop of the vignettes of life in Persia, she declares boldly that the best method of combating the threat of communism in Persia, implied in the move to take control of the country's oil resources, is to help create more jobs through investing in local industries:

[S]ince I came to America I have had businessmen ask me the details of my plan. When I speak of interesting capital they say, "It sounds like an excellent proposition, but—"

The but, I find, is because of several things that have happened in the world very recently. First, maybe is the recent nationalization of the Iranian oil. How can Americans be interested in investing capital where the government at any time may confiscate the properties, or take control of them?

Maybe I am not wise, but I think I have the answer. At least one answer. . . .
Let me tell you about my people. There is much that I do not know, but I do
know the hearts of my people. It is only hunger that can make them listen to
the communists. (224–25)

Interestingly this rationalization is again situated in the rhetoric of intuition.
Having placed Persia in the very core of her own feelings and attachments, she
entitles herself to a close reading of the hearts of all of her compatriots. Even
the humility with which she recognizes the limitations of her experience of the
world is modulated by the confident assertion of her knowledge of Persia and
Persians.

The mingling of hard facts and subjective perceptions is not unlike the
juxtaposition of secrecy and revelation in the presentation of the Najafi family.
In the discussion of Persia's economic dilemmas, the personal hunch is backed
up by the example of Najafi's own professional trajectory before arriving in
the United States. The work she undertook as a small entrepreneur in Tehran
is offered up as a model for Persian economic and social revival.

Najafi's small business, the seamstress shop, called Salon of the Flower,
apparently provided many with jobs and opened her eyes to future possibilities: "What I want to do is to establish in the large village or in a small village
with other villages in the same area, the little factory. Not the great factory
with thousands of humming machines, but the small factory that will employ
the women in productive work. I want them to make simple clothing for men,
women, children, but especially for women" (223). The clumsiness of these
sentences, the unnecessary definite articles in "the great factory" and "the
small factory" like her subtly stated dislike for "thousands of humming machines" place her on the side of authentic cultural values. Yet the paradox of
the plan to bring outside resources to improve conditions within a Persia she
would like to keep more or less intact does not appear to concern her. What
consumes all of her attention is a means of funding her vision: "To carry out
my plan will take very much money. Perhaps I should start with the money I
have saved from my shop, but still I do not know exactly how to begin. I must

go to America for the learning. I will put the problem of the money in the lower drawer of my head until I have time for it" (224). The peculiar image of relegating her future plans to a "drawer" in her mind tells us a great deal about Najafi's selective approach, not only to her own ambitions and career, but also to transculturation as a whole.

Najafi's attitudes to language, culture, and identity are part and parcel of the vision that brings her to America: the means of acquiring necessary tools and props. She treats *The Constitutional History of the United States,* like the bobby socks and the vignettes of family life, as so many props. Like a shrewd salesperson, she offers only what she needs to intrigue potential clients. Selling Persia to American investors is one of the objectives toward which Najafi's efforts at refashioning and adapting are directed.

But not all of her props transfer across the cultural barriers smoothly. Her own language, Persian, poses the greatest difficulty in that it fails to correspond unproblematically to her American audience's needs. She finds it necessary to append a glossary to her book, but she softens its blow by giving it a subtitle, "If You Are Puzzled." The preamble to the glossary nevertheless unveils a frustration she has worked hard to keep in check. Not only have the possessive pronouns crept back in, they are now once again setting up barriers between the Persian and the American:

> I have tried to tell my story in your language, but sometimes there is no single English word that will take the place of one of ours. It is difficult to write these Persian words with the English alphabet. We, too, have an alphabet but our letters and yours are not equivalent. The best I can do is to pronounce the word very carefully and write it with the letters from your alphabet that are nearest the sound. This isn't right, of course, and you can have no real idea of how the words sound spoken, but it is the best I can do. (237)

The sense of irritation is most pronounced when she addresses the lack of equivalents in the letters of the alphabet. She struggles to balance her pride, "We, too, have an alphabet," with the impracticality of the nearest phonetic approximation. Najafi's attempt to sound out Persian words echoes her ease in hearing the Turkish accent of the village headman and transferring herself into his linguistic realm. But English proves more resistant.

Najafi's attempts at transliterating Persian names produce some very interesting results. The name "Zahra" becomes a dyslexic "Zarah": it is the softness of the *h* that makes it almost dispensable or at least endows it with an arbitrary position, while the aspirated *h* in "Mohsen" gets left out altogether and we end up with "Mosen." The name of one of Najafi's sisters becomes distorted from "Fakhri" to "Fahri." For all her worrying about the exact pronunciation of words, the Persian "Isma'il" becomes the more readily recognizable "Ishmael." Most puzzling of all her transliterations of names are "Sijavish," "Sank," and "Ashbage." In the first instance, it is possible to guess "Siavash," but the last two remain a mystery without the glossary.

The haphazard nature of Najafi's transliterations, as she points out in the preface to the glossary, is due to her lack of familiarity with one single transliteration system on which she could draw: "As far as I know, no one has made a standard English spelling of these words. In your books I have seen the name of the Prophet of Islam written: Mohamet, Mohammet, Mohammed, Mohamed" (237). She adds a separate paragraph at the end of the glossary on Persian names: "Persian names are very different from Western names. Perhaps you would like to know how we say those in this story. In Farsi we do not have the heavy accents of the Western languages. In our names each syllable is pronounced with almost the same stress" (243). This is followed by a list of all the names broken down into syllables. Here "Sijavish" transforms itself into "see yah vush" and "Zarah" becomes "Zah rah." Apart from the breakdown of syllables this pronunciation guide reveals that she could have easily adopted its system in the body of the narrative. She seemed to have constrained herself unnecessarily with a less adequate set of equivalents—a problem she does resolve in her next two books. For instance, in *A Wall and Three Willows,* "Mosen" is transformed into "Mohsen," and in *Reveille for a Persian Village,* "Zahra" replaces the "Zarah" of *Persia Is My Heart.* The linguistic hurdles Najafi has no desire to overcome are reminders of the essential cultural differences she is intent on preserving.

Beyond the transliteration of Persian words, Najafi emphasizes the near impossibility of translating Persian into English: "What the poets have written the people have memorized and have taught their children from one generation to another. Perhaps it is because Farsi is a beautiful *liquid* language. I have been told that it is even more beautiful than Italian and not to be compared with the harshness of English. In our language we do not have a jolting combination of stressed and unstressed syllables, rather there is a softness in each syllable. Farsi is the language of poetry" (emphasis added, 109–10). Interestingly, at her most intuitive, she slips back into referring to her language as Farsi and fails to find adequate words and phrases in English. The missing natural flow of her language, its "liquidity" and "softness," are opposed to the "jolting" syllables and "harshness" of English. Like other ideas she has clearly formed before leaving Persia, her aversion to the sound of English dates back to her encounters with English while still at home.

Already before arriving in the United States, she confesses, the sound of English she used to hear at her seamstress shop did not appeal to her: "I did not like the loud voices of the English and American women, the dull drop, like lead, of the voice at the end of each sentences, the exaggerated inflection, the wide range of pitch of their voices. I like the Persian voice, soft, with an upward lift at the end of the sentences" (204). Worth noting is her switching back to the use of the term "Persian." This is at least in part due to the fact that the discussion no longer is focused on her passion for the sounds of her own language. As if to protect her "beautiful liquid language" from possible contamination by English, she renders it back into Persian. That she relates to language as immutable and fixed is evident in her essentialization of languages other than Persian and English.

Among Western languages, she finds French has more affinities with Persian. When discussing literature she has read in translation, she says: "There is something in the French temperament and the Persian temperament that is particularly congenial. Translations from the French are not word translations; they are something more" (109). It is not the French language per se that she finds more congenial and appealing, but rather the translations of French she has read in Persian: "In excellent translation we have the works of

Victor Hugo. *Les Miserables* I loved to read over and over. Jean Valjean was my brother. He knew hunger for bread as I had seen it in my country. He had made a life of giving, and he had improved the condition of those around him" (108). In this light, the notion of French translations not being "word translations" would appear to imply that, as a language, French is capable of expressing sentiments she finds close to Persian, or as she makes explicit in the next passage, *her* sensibilities. Reading and rereading Hugo's work rekindles her own passions: "And the dream I had had of helping the people of the village came back to me. For a time I had almost forgotten it" (109). French, as filtered through a translation that reminds her of her own dreams and plans, can be endowed with the "something more" that is missing from English.

In the absence of this "something more," Najafi goes on with approximations she tries to infuse with extra vigor. Here is how, in a segment from "Myself," she describes Persian cuisine: *"Horisht* is really our word for gravy—but such gravy! The principal ingredient is chicken, fried or steamed, or perhaps lamb, infrequently beef. . . . After an hour of slow simmering the chicken or meat is added to the sauce and allowed to stand long enough to take on its delicious flavour. This is horisht, and served with polo it is the best tasting food in the world" (23). Persian food, like literature and culture, is another means of maintaining the uniqueness of the new nation she embodies.

Such moments of unqualified excess in which she gives free rein to her sense of enthusiasm for things Persian do not distract Najafi from her primary goal: reaching out to potential American sponsors. For instance, the passage in which she complains about the harshness of English she used to overhear in her shop is immediately followed by a reminder of her own practical approach to business: "But I served all the women. There was money coming in to give me a fund for some important project" (204).

The journey away from her homeland, though integral to Najafi's larger plan for bringing about social change, is ultimately subordinated to Najafi's focus on her identity and, by extension, Persian identity. The time she spends in the United States and the changes she has to undergo during that period become brief moments, or vignettes in her narrative. The image of her in the library, dressed in American 1950s style, occupies a prominent position in the opening pages of *Persia Is My Heart,* but it serves to underline the contrast between Najmeh's appearance and her inner affinities with Persia.

Reveille for a Persian Village opens with another such vignette. The book begins with her return journey. In fact, it is the only example of a moment of passage throughout the three works and it expresses a momentary suspension between states and identities: "Far beneath our plane, the greenness of Lebanon merged into the sandy sweeps of Iraq. The man beside me closed his magazine and leaned forward to look out past me. After a moment he settled back again, apparently determined to find something more interesting inside the plane than out" (1). The something more interesting, not altogether surprisingly, turns out to be the woman sitting next to him. Moreover, because the narrator has already long before determined his identity as an American, she is in control of the dialogue that ensues. In this manner, although suspended in midair between two countries, Najafi succeeds in erasing all traces of hesitation and indeterminacy.

The conversation, in fact, turns around the issue of identity and brings to light, despite Najmeh's slowness in divulging her nationality ("I knew he thought that I was Lebanese" (1), her desire to do away with this temporary statelessness and settle back into the realm of familiarity. Although she does not particularly want to encourage a dialogue with the stranger, she does respond grudgingly: " 'I am going home to Teheran' " (1). To the fellow passenger's persistent inquiries about possible acquaintances she might have made during her four years in the United States and which might tempt her back, she replies: " 'Iran's my country' " (2). The stranger's " 'H'm, a four years' journey!' " prompts even further reflection, on her part, on the nature of her journey: "And I thought, I wonder what he would say if I told him that I have really been on this same journey for twenty years; ever since my nurse Zahra, took me into a hungry village and I knew deep inside myself that someday, sometime, I must do something for my country. This feeling had come again and again to me, as I grew up in Teheran, as I visited the villages, as I decided to study in America, and as I attended classes there, gaining the skills I would need to work with my people" (2). The messianic tone of this passage does, at first, detract from its depiction of how Najafi's journey away from home is redirected toward goals on which she had settled while living in Persia. The chronology she provides of her life also makes her four years away from home into a stage in her return. What is emphasized is the return rather than her having been away. With this renewed focus, she can venture into a discussion of her accomplishments after her return.

Following this logic, *Reveille for a Persian Village* and *A Wall and Three Willows* revolve around the fruit of her successes. In them, she acknowledges the financial support she received through various agencies such as the Ford and the Near East Foundation. In fact, the work she was able to undertake with these funds constitutes the focus of these two narratives. Her own life, her marriage to a Persian man, who follows in her footsteps and goes to the United States for a course of study, the birth of her two children, are interwoven into her trajectory as a social worker. This is not a radical departure from her approach in *Persia Is My Heart,* but, in the later works, her voice deviates from the subtle play of internal recognition and alienation. Although she had once chosen not to dwell on the differences between herself and villagers in Azerbaijan, after returning to her homeland she has a tendency to posit villagers as objects of her attention and care.

This propensity is much more noticeable in *A Wall and Three Willows,* where she begins to occupy the position of an outsider vis-à-vis the Baluchis she has agreed to help. For instance, when asked if she speaks Baluchi, she reflects: "Baluchi! One of the dialects both like and unlike the Farsi of most of Iran. In the dialects of the remote tribes the Indo-European root words are still maintained. Baluchi. Almost a new language. This I must learn since talking to women through an interpreter is like speaking through a veil" (1967, 25). The way in which she juxtaposes "like" and "unlike" in her comparison of Baluchi and Persian evokes some of the parallels she had drawn in the scene of her encounter with the Azerbaijani village headman. In contrast to the surprise she experienced in the earlier episode, however, her approach to Baluchi is more clearly marked by a sense of distance. Needless to say, Baluchi does not wield the same power in her imagination as Turkish. In the case of Baluchi, recognition of certain words and familiar linguistic patterns is not rewarding enough to get her beyond the initial hurdles of communication. Her linguistic alienation is underlined in the curious remark, "almost a new language," by which she probably means new to her, and the possibility of the need for an interpreter. Although she decides against using a linguistic intermediary, Najafi does not succeed completely in removing the veil separating her from the villagers.

The gap that we see opening up in this admission that she would have to approach Baluchi much in the same manner as she would any foreign language widens even more after her arrival in Baluchistan: "I had known that work in Baluchistan would be difficult—but I had not known the strength of the wall that these *primitive* people would build against us. They felt that they had no need for us; that we were intruders. For centuries without number they had managed without the aid of 'foreigners.' It would take all of our imagination and persistence to find an opening for ourselves" (emphasis added, 29). Feeling rejected by the very people she has come to help transforms Najafi, in her own eyes, into an intruder and foreigner. As a wall is erected between her and the Baluchis, she identifies more closely with the Persian and the American social workers who share her values and concerns. This mechanism of identification is reflected in her use of pronouns: she switches from "I" to "we," as *Reveille for a Persian Village* and *A Wall and Three Willows* become testimonies of the collective and community achievements in which Najafi participates. This community now includes American aid workers and generous donors, who are cited in the glossary, still called "If You are Puzzled," appended to *Reveille for a Persian Village*. Under the heading of "About American Assistance to the People of Iran," she writes: "Many people who hear about the problems of my country ask, 'What are *we* doing to help?' A brief answer may lead those who are interested into further study" (1958, 270).

This change in Najafi's cultural affiliations clashes with her persistent desire to identify with all Persian villagers. That she finds it necessary to distance herself from the Baluchi villagers is indicative of the shifts in her notion of Persian identity. To be Persian now means embracing the idea of progress and modernization. Gone is the urge to preserve native authenticity that was evident in *Persia Is My Heart*. Interestingly, Najafi's "decorations" that accompanied her first work are replaced, first by "decorations" by another Persian in *Reveille for a Persian Village,* which also provides some photographs, and finally, by photographs only, in *A Wall and Three Willows.* This marks a shift away from the need to evoke Persia as a mysterious and exotic realm to which American readers gain access through Najafi's words. The focus of the story is redirected in the later works to the need to document the work of transforming Persian village life.

Najafi's tone and approach have both evolved from the naïve and tentative outlines of *Persia Is My Heart,* a change Helen Hinckley notes at the end of *A Wall and Three Willows:* "It differs from the other two books in that Najmeh has matured, her outlook has been changed somewhat by this maturing, and the dreams that were only dreams in the first two books are fulfilled" (13). There is a curious link between Najafi's maturity and her closer identification with transformations of Persia from "primitive" to a modernized state. Najafi herself alludes to this in the final paragraph of the glossary, "Operation Sarbandan": "My work in the awakening of one small group of villages has been assisted by many of these agencies and by my friends. Since the royalties from *Persia Is My Heart* and from *Reveille for a Persian Village* go directly into this work, many of you have been direct contributors toward making life more livable for those who happened to have been born in a land of undiscovered, undeveloped opportunities" (1958, 273). This marks the achievement of Najafi's professional goals. She set out to acquire American sympathy and support for her projects and the evidence she provides seems to point to success. But are her books merely reports of accomplishments and expressions of gratitude?

As I have suggested in my analysis of *Persia Is My Heart,* Najmeh Najafi's accounts of selfless dedication to improving the lot of Persian villagers allow us glimpses, however oblique they might be, of the types of identities she stages for her audiences. In *Persia Is My Heart,* we see her playing at becoming American. She studies and dresses the part in order to convince her readers that her compatriots are capable of adapting to the broader changes that modernization would demand of them, were the wealthier nations to become interested in the project of Westernizing Persia. Throughout this performance, Najafi believes in her ability to keep her Persian self intact. The very title of her first work and the clumsiness of her English sentences anchor her in this identity. If she writes with an accent, in the sense Taghi Modarressi delineates in what he calls the "artifact" voice of an immigrant or an exile writer (1992, 9), it is not with an awareness of the extent to which her mingling of her "liquid" Persian with the "harshness" of English is already changing her perceptions of herself and her compatriots. Elements of this longing to preserve her imagined identity are evident in the works written after her return home.

In the villages, she teaches other women how to become independent and self-reliant, but she is still reluctant to step outside societal expectations. She observes local customs in an attempt to leave the life of the villages as undisturbed as possible. But alongside this adherence to tradition, she also sees herself, or is perceived by the villagers, as an outsider. It is not the presence of this tension that is noteworthy, but rather Najafi's struggle to resolve it by insisting on the possibility of maintaining Persianness at a safe distance from intrusions from outside Persian borders. As her own dressing up in the proper American costume manifests, she is convinced that no more than cosmetic changes are needed to attain better material conditions. The paradoxical question at the very core of her venture is whether dressed for America, she can recapture the Persia that was her heart.

The answer is implied in the very manner in which Najafi and her American collaborator depict her personal progress through the stages of her careful journey into the land of opportunity, her acquiring enough material and knowledge to help her compatriots, and her return to a secure and grounded sense of being Persian. Unlike the nineteenth-century merchant, Mu'in al-Saltanah, however, Najafi's identity is more heavily encumbered by artifice. Her need to demonstrate how her country has benefited from her discoveries abroad points to the impossibility of keeping Persia secure from outside "contamination."

Najafi's dream of mesmerizing audiences with her talent and charms might be realized on one level. She presents us with a carefully choreographed identity, aimed at highlighting the effortlessness with which a Persian can acquire the trappings of modern life. Yet, at the end of her performance, we are left wondering how long the accent, the wardrobe, and the choreography can be sustained. All her claims of successful and proud accomplishments cannot eradicate the signs of rupture within the concept of a modern nation.

As we have seen, Al-e Ahmad, one of the leading intellectuals of this era, seizes upon these inner contradictions and depicts them as a disease:

> I speak of being afflicted with "westitis" the way I would speak of being afflicted with cholera. If this is not palatable let us say it is akin to being stricken by heat or by cold. But it is not that either. It is something more on the order of being attacked by tongue worm. Have you ever seen how wheat rots? From within. The husk remains whole, but it is only an empty shell like the discarded chrysalis of a butterfly hanging from a tree. In any case, we are dealing with a sickness, a disease imported from abroad, and developed in an environment receptive to it. Let us discover the characteristics of this illness and its cause or causes and, if possible, find a cure (1982, 3).

The cures Al-e Ahmad and other intellectuals sought were intended to restore national honor and integrity, concepts that carry highly gendered connotations and continue to affirm binary divisions of insider/outsider and self/other. The healing practice Al-e Ahmad and other leading intellectuals of this era advocated called for containment of what was perceived as external influence. But efforts toward this end, as demonstrated in the most recent chapters of Persian history, have far from resolved the contradictions that have beset modern Persian cultural identity. Dreams of purism and essentialism have produced equally fraught fictions of identity. That gender and the body have become sites for discipline and regulation confirms the persistence of the problematic we have observed in the last two chapters. Women, it would seem, still bear the burden of saving the nation from its malaise.

Conclusion

I began this book with an intuitive and, perhaps, naïve assumption that reading Persian narratives of encounter with the West would help me better grasp my own transcultural journey and, by extension, the place of such encounters in the ever-changing patterns of the Persian discourses of identity. What inspired my inquiry was not so much the need to demonstrate that Persians, like their European and American counterparts, had observed and analyzed cultures and peoples unknown to them. This work has been masterfully accomplished by scholars who have engaged with images of the West in Persian literature, historical narrative, and intellectual movements. This scholarship has informed every stage of my analysis.

My aim has been to begin with the smaller units of identity, the life at the center of the Persian stories of encounter with the West. The absence of a confessional mode of self-representation in Persian has frustrated literary critics and has led to the conclusion that the genre of autobiography does not exist in Persian letters. This apparent lack has in turn forestalled the possibility of examining the conditions and parameters of the existing modes of self-narration. If Persians relate the self only to the broader units of community and nation, is it to be assumed that these manifestations of the self are not worthy of analysis and a place in the history of culture and letters? The answer I have sketched out in the preceding five chapters suggests that the seemingly depersonalized accounts of life and travels can tell us much about the narrating self and its struggles with conflicting cultural archives. The personal stories that emerge at the intersections of memoirs, diaries, and sociohistorical narratives are part and parcel of the cultural history we have come to equate with prominent literati and intellectuals. By turning to less important characters and their stories, I have endeavored to take a step away from a tradition of scholarship that replicates the belief that cultural history is written by larger-than-life figures. In my introduction I stated that the history of a literature is also the history of its criticism. Disinheriting the types of writing that refuse to fit into existing definitions and generic criteria prevents our collective scholarly community from grappling with the persistence of the desire to record life histories. If Persian lives continue to be written, they must speak to an audience whose expectations are different from the ones the critics bring to bear on their readings. I would suggest that we begin to read differently. In the paradoxical juxtaposition of the need to conform to imperatives of personal modesty and the tendency toward self-aggrandizement, for instance, we might uncover signs of a struggle to articulate the self both within and outside the communal frame of reference. The ways in which these competing demands play themselves out determine the form and style of narratives that together make up the history of Persian understandings of the self. But even this approach will not be able to construct a definitive truth of the self, for self-discovery and self-construction are complex processes that will always leave traces of concealment and disavowal.

Having reached the end of my readings of the five characters around whom I have organized the chapters of my book, I am conscious of all that I left out of the personal narrative I sketched out in my introduction. It is precisely my prying into the lives of these Persians that has brought me face to face with many untold parts of my own story. In this conclusion, then, I want to return to what I have held back and attempt to weave it together with what has emerged in the five preceding chapters.

The account of the seventeenth-century Persian embassy's difficult departure from the shores of the Caspian Sea, especially their inadvertent return to Persia, reminded me of my own first, aborted, though not altogether voluntary, leave-taking from Persia at the age of sixteen.

Like my sister who, a year before me, had won an exchange scholarship to spend her last year of high school with a family in the United States, I too had passed the tests and been placed with an American family in Connecticut. But, unlike my sister, I was disinclined to leave home. Winning a scholarship was one thing, spending a year away from family and friends altogether different. The seminars and sessions intended to prepare our group for life in the United States had only confirmed my worst fears about the changes I would have to undertake.

I spent a restless night before the scheduled dawn flight, fantasizing about all manner of unforeseen interruptions and cancellations of my trip. Dragging my suitcase and myself at the Tehran airport, I was still lost in these fantasies when it was announced that not all of the students could be accommodated on that day's flight and our trip would be postponed by a day. I took this to be a providential affirmation of my own hesitation to leave. Much more joyous than the other students and the relatives who had come to see us off and would have to wake up at the crack of dawn one more time, I was determined to enjoy every second of this blessed return to the security of family.

Like Uruch Beg's companions who, once unexpectedly returned to Persian soil, wanted to disembark and return to their normal lives, I too entertained the idea of not showing up at the airport the next morning. To my chagrin, no one would take my broad hints for anything but idle chatter. The flight left on time the following day, and, like Uruch Beg, I have never been able to retrace my steps to the home I left so reluctantly. Like the seventeenth-century convert, I too have tried to get beyond the anguish of that first departure. In fact, at certain moments, I have boldly claimed that I have never looked back and could no longer relate to the anxieties of that early morning in August 1975.

We need these rewritings of painful ruptures in our past in order to create new lives for ourselves. When I read this declaration in Don Juan of Persia— "I soon discovered that, being now a Christian, the conversation of my Persian fellow countrymen, with whom I had heretofore been on terms of inseparable comradeship, was now no longer in any sense to my taste" (303)—I hear myself saying, "I can't stand the Persian immigrant ghettos; all that desperate clinging to the past makes me claustrophobic." Well hidden behind my impatience and irritability is the recognition of loss of an unquestioned allegiance to a fixed notion of home, language, and culture. Losing myself in my maternal relatives' legend of shuttling across borders, I have tried to convince myself, at various points in my life, of the importance of believing in nomadic movement. Yet, I would have to confess that there are still moments when I envy friends with deep roots in one place. During those periods, I feel equally impatient with my life in Canada. I have recently heard myself say: "I am tired of the customs of this country."

This desire to be at once part of and detached from my adopted home has played itself out in strange ways through the twenty some years I have lived in Canada. At every sign of a possible separation of Quebec from the rest of Canada, I become a fervent nationalist, holding forth on the need to preserve Canada's linguistic and cultural diversity. Returning to Canada from trips abroad, I have sensed immense relief at slipping back into familiar patterns and customs. But I have also been known to take offense at well-intentioned compliments on my English. "Where did you learn to speak such good English?" gets my hackles up and instantly returns me to my Persian communal identity. I wonder why my Canadian compatriots should assume that we, Persians, would not be able to master their tongue.

This kind of renewed pride on my part echoes both Mu'in al-Saltanah's impregnable identification with Persia and Persians and 'Abdullah Mustawfi's anxieties about full compliance with European manners. On a deeper level, this reminds me of the missing middle part of my own story: how I learned English. I am conscious of the fact that, like Mustawfi, I have glossed over the agonies I experienced in that first year in Connecticut. It is by way of those missing chapters of my life that I want to establish links to the stories of the missing Persians I have been writing about.

Unlike Mustawfi, I did not have the luxury of cloistering myself in a study and reading up on American customs. Having fully internalized the nuances of English grammar, I arrived in the States to discover that my bookish knowledge did not in any way correspond to the pace of the spoken language. Because the exchange students spent a few days in Long Island before being shipped out to the awaiting families, I was not immediately immersed in the sense of panic that overtook me the minute I stepped off the bus in New London. Even the sweet smiles on the faces of the four members of the McCausland family could not compensate for the dread I felt at not being able to catch the words whizzing by me. On the drive home, fatigue, homesickness, and panic worked their peculiar alchemy to produce a bizarre numbness that two days later gave way to an uncontrollable bout of crying. Alfred, Betty, Libby, and Scott McCausland did their best to calm my frayed nerves; little did they know that the barrage of their words of solace was precisely what I was crying about. What kept running through my head was an image of heavy chests of English words I was going to have to tap into in the two weeks I had before school started. The image itself had an alarming link to a nightmare I had had the first day we began learning the multiplication tables in elementary school. That night I woke up from a terrifying dream in which four monstrous-looking men were packing the multiplication tables into crates and secreting them away. My screaming to stop the thieves brought my parents to my bedside. My father, who never had a passion for numbers, reassured me that the multiplication tables, alas, were beyond pilfering and interpreted my dream to mean I shared his loathing of math. Comforting as his interpretation was that night, at the return of the image of crates full of words in Connecticut I could only draw up one conclusion: my secret aversion to English. That my father was a committed Francophile played no small part in my extrapolations.

Aside from the linguistic quandary, I found out, somewhat like Muʿin al-Saltanah, that I had an inflexible palate. If in an Italian village he asked for *khaginih,* a Persian variety of scrambled eggs, and, finding out the Italians had never heard of the dish, set about making it himself, on my first morning at the McCausland home, I would have been happy to have been given a chance to make my own breakfast. To my horror, I was served a bowl of cereal floating in milk, my least favorite food. It took no more than two spoonfuls for the family to come to my rescue. This trial by milk inadvertently produced the right effect; my next challenge, learning English, I realized would be far more palatable.

So I began the slow and formidable task of picking up words and phrases. Like Mustawfi, I became obsessed with getting everything right. Mastery of slang, especially of the teenage variety, was my ultimate challenge. I tuned my ears to every turn of phrase my American friends used in high school. Yet, all this hard work did not necessarily pay off. Try as I might, I could not step into the frame of mind that enabled my class mates to carry their bodies around with a strange combination of ease and abandon. Even those occasions on which I said the right words were filled with a thorough sense of alienation. That I would never fit in was confirmed to me when my own American sister, Libby McCausland, one day declared to me that I did not know how to have fun.

Thinking about Libby's statement, in light of my reading of Mustawfi's ordeals at the St Petersburg luncheon on January 6, 1905, I realize how very accurate her assessment was. My behavior was not all that different from Mustawfi's. So absorbed was he in the observance of proper etiquette that he could not enjoy the many courses of delicacies served at the luncheon. All his worrying about what to do with the printed menu, how to make the right kind of small talk, and how to prove himself an equal to the other Europeans dignitaries transformed the state luncheon into a rite of passage. Like Mustawfi, in Connecticut I felt I could never let my guard down. I was on a mission whose object was a complete makeover of myself. I too found no room for personal pleasure.

Six years ago when I visited Scott McCausland and his wife at their home in Portland, I was taken aback by his asking me where and when I learned to speak English. Was not the answer obvious to him? He was there all those minutes, hours, and days of my stumbling around, desperately searching for the right word and pronunciation. Amazingly, he had no memory of my not being able to speak English, hence his assumption that he and I had always been on an equal footing.

The differences in Scott's and my recollections of the year I lived with them in Connecticut made me realize how so carefully we sometimes disguise the difficulties we encounter in the course of our transcultural passages and how easily the unpleasant memories can be evoked.

Quite recently, years after my first struggles with English, I was at a small gathering with a few friends and colleagues. Late in the evening, about the time when I would normally let my guard down, I made a linguistic slip and said, "I was sleeping at the wheel." A colleague cheerfully offered: "No you were asleep at the wheel." This simple and friendly correction produced an instantaneous chain reaction and brought back to me a whole list of such mistakes I had made over the years. With this private dictionary of malapropisms floating through my head, I remembered the acute sense of defeat I experienced every time I made mistakes during my first years of learning English.

My most unsettling moments of linguistic anxiety have revolved around illness. Waiting for a major operation in a hospital room some years ago, I displaced my anxieties onto what would happen in the post-op. My primary concern was whether I would be able to understand the nurses and doctors. My fears proved to be unfounded, but, as I was regaining consciousness, I did struggle with words. Over and above the pain and grogginess was a stubborn unwillingness to answer the nurse's questions. Feeling vulnerable, I could not muster the energy to articulate answers to simple questions about how I felt and whether I could remember my date of birth. At that moment, all I could think about was how tired I was of speaking English. I missed abandoning myself to a language that did not demand of me full consciousness and control.

Back in the hospital room, I recovered my linguistic faculties faster than the visible scars, forever reminding me of how life-giving forces had been neatly carved out of my body, would heal. The surgical tape covering the stitches became for me a metaphor of the precariously held together transcultural person I had become over the years. I followed the surgeon's orders and gingerly ambled up and down the hospital halls, but not without a constant, albeit unfounded, fear that the tapes and stitches would come undone. At some level, I understood that I was worried about the kind of unraveling I had imagined myself experiencing in the post-op. I could take comfort in the fact that I had not lost my command of English. Yet I had embarked on a path toward learning an inner language of loss.

I see certain affinities between these reminders of my not having a native, intuitive grasp of English and the opening scene of Najmeh Najafi's *Persia Is My Heart*. Dressed in an American outfit, sitting at a library, and reading about the history of the United States, she is painfully conscious of not blending in with the rest of the scene. She too stumbles over words and closes the book on the pretense of being American by declaring, "even in America Persia is my heart."

I am barred from the path taken by Najafi because I cannot maintain the illusion that there is an easy route back to home for me. This is not a veiled allusion to all that has happened in my country of birth in recent decades, but rather a recognition that I too have changed and am missing some of what once made Persia home. Coming face to face with these changes is the worst kind of homesickness I have experienced.

When I returned home in 1989, after an absence of twelve years, I felt a peculiar brand of alienation. Here I was in a country whose language I knew inside out, whose geography and history were thoroughly familiar to me. And, yet, I could not fit in the landscape of my erstwhile home. There were plenty of visible changes to which I could attribute my malaise, but it was the lack of correspondence between my own memories and the person I had become that was at the root of my sense of exile. I understood this only on my way out of the country. Waiting in the departure hall of the airport, I approached a couple to ask for a light to smoke a cigarette. My very polite question went unanswered for what seemed to me like minutes. Finally the husband fumbled around for his lighter and offered me a light. As he was lighting my cigarette, he complimented me on my fluency in Persian. Few foreigners, he had come across, spoke Persian so well. It was my turn to fumble around and find something adequately civil to offer by way of response. I thanked him in a hurry and said that I was a native speaker of Persian. Clearly both of us were disappointed with the turn our conversation had taken. As we parted ways, uttering phrases we knew instinctively, I was left grieving for the teenager I had been in 1975. I would have known this grief even if I had never left home.

Of the five figures I have discussed, Taj al-Saltanah best grasps and articulates this sense of division within. She did not have to leave Persia in order to understand her internal ruptures she found echoed in her readings of European history and literature. The shadowy self she uncovered through study and reflection, about which she wrote courageously, mirrors my own and the other missing Persians' unarticulated fears of facing the other within. If she leaves us with more contradictions than resolutions, it is because confrontations of the sort we have experienced resist tidy closures. But, from between the cracks and fissures, there emerge voices that cannot go unheeded. These voices, however, discordant they might be, are and will remain integral parts of the multitude of Persian identities that form the seemingly homogeneous notions of who we are and how we interact with others living beyond the real and imagined borders of Persia.

It is not merely my own transculturation that makes me insist on this cacophony of Persian voices. As the story of my childhood reveals, long before crossing into other lands and cultures, my map of Persia included a wide array of languages, ethnicities, and cultures. Ironically, away from home, I have sometimes framed Persian identity along the lines of linguistic uniformity. When I meet other Persians in Canada, I speak to them in Persian first. Other languages we might share, like Gilaki or Azari, become secondary in the process of establishing common ties. Linguistic differences aside, I would suggest that the many fragmented voices that have emerged through *Missing Persians* are equally significant building blocks for what we call Persianness. Going away from Persia has been historically a fruitful means of coming to terms with native and national identity. We have not always resisted outside impetus and input. At certain moments, we have sought them out and engaged constructively with the manners, customs, and laws of other peoples and cultures. In fact, journeying away from the self as a means of grasping it resonates within Persian poetic tradition. Like the birds in Farid al-Din 'Attar's *Conference of the Birds* who set out in search of the legendary *Simurgh* only to find him within themselves, Persian travelers have sometimes ended their arduous journeys in self-discovery.

My desire to insert these fives voices into Persian literary and cultural history is deeply rooted in the narrative of my life. I see myself as one of those missing Persians who wants to leave some trace of the process that has led to sitting at the crossroads of many languages and cultures. The value I attach to these narratives of Persian encounter with the West, I hope, goes beyond their literary merit. In fact, in no way have I provided systematic answers to questions about their place within the Western literary genres. Ultimately it matters little what labels we apply to these texts. They do not need to be carefully categorized as either autobiography, memoir, or travel literature to be read as instances of lives written into Persian cultural history. *Missing Persians* is an invitation to others to find stories such as those told by Uruch Beg, Mu'in al-Saltanah, Mustawfi, and Najafi and to further explore their place in our collective cultural imagination.

Works Cited

Index

Works Cited

Adams, Percy G. 1983. *Travel Literature and the Evolution of the Novel.* Lexington: Univ. Press of Kentucky.

Afary, Janet. 1996. *The Iranian Constitutional Revolution, 1906–1911: Grassroots Democracy, Social Democracy, and the Origins of Feminism.* New York: Columbia Univ. Press.

Al-e Ahmad, Jalal. 1982. *Plagued by the West.* Translated by Paul Sprachman. Delmar, N.Y.: Caravan.

Amanat, 'Abbas. 1993. Introduction to *Crowning Anguish: Memoirs of a Persian Princess from the Harem to Modernity 1884–1914,* by Taj Al-Santana. Translated by Anna Vanzan and Amin Neshati. Washington, D.C.: Mage.

Anderson, Benedict. 1991. *Imagined Communities: Reflections on the Origin and Spread of Nationalism.* 1983. Reprint, London: Verso.

Anzaldúa, Gloria. 1987. *Borderlands/La Frontera: The New Mestiza.* San Francisco: Aunt Lute Books.

Apter, Emily. 1995. "Comparative Exile: Competing Margins in the History of Comparative Literature." In *Comparative Literature in the Age of Multiculturalism,* edited by Charles Bernheimer, 86–96. Baltimore: Johns Hopkins Univ. Press.

Ashraf, Ahmad. 1996. "Tarikh, Khatirih, Afsanih." *Iran Nameh* 14, no. 4: 525–38.

Atabaki, Touraj. 1993. *Azerbaijan: Ethnicity and Autonomy in Twentieth-Century Iran.* London: British Academy Press.

Avery, Peter. 1965. *Modern Iran.* New York: Praeger.

Balaÿ, Christophe. 1999. *Paydayish-i Roman-i Farsi.* Translated by Mahvash Qavimi and Nasrin Khattat. Tehran: Mu'in.

Bancroft, Hubert Howe, ed. 1893. *The Book of the Fair: An Historical and Descriptive Presentation of the World's Science, Art, and Industry as Viewed Through the Columbian Exposition at Chicago in 1893.* Section 5. Chicago: Bancroft.

Barthold, W. 1984. *An Historical Geography of Iran.* Translated by Svat Soucek. Princeton: Princeton Univ. Press.

Boroujerdi, Mehrzad. 1996. *Iranian Intellectuals and the West: The Tormented Triumph of Nativism.* Syracuse: Syracuse Univ. Press.

Browne, Edward G. 1959. *A Literary History of Persia.* Vol. 4. 1924. Reprint, Cambridge: Cambridge Univ. Press.

Chaqueri, Cosroe. 1995. *The Soviet Socialist Republic of Iran 1920–1921: Birth of the Trauma.* Pittsburgh: Univ. of Pittsburgh Press.

Cole, Juan R. I. 1996. "Marking Boundaries, Marking Time: The Iranian Past and the Construction of the Self by Qajar Thinkers." *Iranian Studies* 29, nos. 1–2: 35–56.

Cortés, D. Narciso Alonso, ed. 1946. *Relaciones de Don Juan de Persia.* Madrid: Gráficas Ultra.

Dabashi, Hamid. 1985. "The Poetics of Politics: Commitment in Modern Persian Literature." *Iranian Studies* 18, nos. 2–4: 147–88.

Deleuze, Gilles, and Félix Guattari. 1986. *Kafka: Toward a Minor Literature.* Translated by Dana Polan. Minneapolis: Univ. of Minnesota Press.

Egerton, George. 1994. *Political Memoir: Essays on the Politics of Memory.* London: Frank Cass.

Eslami-Nodushan, Mohammad 'Ali. 1969. "The Influence of Europe on Literary Modernization in Iran." *Middle East Journal* 23: 529–34.

Foucault, Michel. 1990. *History of Sexuality: An Introduction.* Vol. 1. Translated by Robert Hurley. New York: Vintage.

Fragner, Bert G. 1979. *Persische Memoirenliteratur als Quelle zur neueren Geschichte Irans.* Wiesbaden: Franz Steiner.

Garber, Marjorie. 1992. *Vested Interests: Cross-Dressing and Cultural Anxiety.* New York: Routledge.

Ghanoonparvar, M. R. 1993. *In a Persian Mirror: Images of the West and Westerners in Iranian Fiction.* Austin: Univ. of Texas Press.

Gheissari, Ali. 1998. *Iranian Intellectuals in the Twentieth Century.* Austin: Univ. of Texas Press.

Goldman, Anne E. 1998. "Autobiography, Ethnography, and History: A Model for

Reading." In *Women, Autobiography, Theory: A Reader,* edited by Sidonie Smith and Julia Watson, 288–98. Madison: Univ. of Wisconsin Press.

Gusdorf, Georges. 1980. "Conditions and Limits of Autobiography." In *Autobiography: Essays Theoretical and Critical,* edited by James Olney, 28–48. Princeton: Princeton Univ. Press.

Hanaway, William L. 1990. "Half-Voices: Persian Women's Lives and Letters." In *Women's Autobiographies in Contemporary Iran,* edited by Afsaneh Najmabadi, 55–63. Harvard Middle Eastern Monographs 25. Cambridge, Mass.: Harvard Univ. Press.

———. N.d. "Persian Travel Narratives: Notes Toward the Definition of a Nineteenth-Century Genre." Unpublished paper.

Hinckley, Helen, and Najmeh Najafi. 1953. *Persia Is My Heart.* New York: Harper & Brothers.

———. 1958. *Reveille for a Persian Village.* New York: Harper.

———. 1967. *A Wall and Three Willows.* New York: Harper & Row.

Kadar, Marlene. 1992. *Essays on Life Writing: From Genre to Critical Practice.* Toronto: Univ. of Toronto Press.

Kamshad, Hasan. 1966. *Modern Persian Prose Literature.* Cambridge: Cambridge Univ. Press.

Kaplan, Caren. 1992. "Resisting Autobiography: Out-Law Genres and Transnational Feminist Subjects." In *De/Colonizing the Subject: The Politics of Gender in Women's Autobiography,* edited by Sidonie Smith and Julia Watson, 115–38. Minneapolis: Univ. of Minnesota Press.

Kramer, Martin. 1991. "Introduction." In *Middle Eastern Lives: The Practice of Biography and Self-Narrative,* edited by Martin Kramer, 1–19. Syracuse: Syracuse Univ. Press.

Lambton, Ann K. S. 1987. *Qajar Persia: Eleven Studies.* Austin: Univ. of Texas Press.

Le Strange, Guy, trans. and ed. 1973. *Don Juan of Persia: A Shi'ah Catholic 1560–1604.* 1926. Reprint. New York: Arno Press.

Levy, Reuben. 1969. *An Introduction to Persian Literature.* New York: Columbia Univ. Press.

Lockhart, Laurence. 1997. "European Contacts with Persia, 1350–1736." In *The Cambridge History of Iran.* Vol. 6, edited by Peter Jackson and Laurence Lockhart, 373–409. 1986. Reprint. Cambridge: Cambridge Univ. Press.

Mathee, Rudi. 1998. "Between Aloofness and Fascination: Safavid Views of the West." *Iranian Studies* 31, no. 2: 219–46.

Meisami, Julie Scott. 1987. *Medieval Persian Court Poetry*. Princeton: Princeton Univ. Press.

Meskoob, Shahrokh. 1992. *Iranian Nationality and the Persian Language*. Translated by Michael Hillmann. Washington, D.C.: Mage.

Milani, Farzaneh. 1987. "The Memoirs of Taj-O Saltaneh." *Iranian Studies* 19, no. 2: 188–93.

———. 1992. *Veils and Words: The Emerging Voices of Iranian Women Writers*. Syracuse: Syracuse Univ. Press.

Modarressi, Taghi. 1992. "Writing with an Accent." *Chanteh* 1:7–9.

Montesquieu. 1973. *Persian Letters*. Translated by C. J. Betts. Toronto: Penguin.

Mu'in al-Saltanah. 1982. *Safarnamih-i Shikagu: Khatirat-i Haji Muhammad 'Ali Mu'in al-Saltanah bih Urupa va Amrika*. Edited by Humayun Shahidi. Tehran: Intisharat-i 'Ilmi.

Mustawfi, 'Abdullah. 1982. *Sharh-i Zindigani-yi Man*. 3 vols. Tehran: Zavvar.

Mottahedeh, Roy. 1985. *The Mantle of the Prophet: Religion and Politics in Iran*. New York: Pantheon.

Najmabadi, Afsaneh. 1990. "A Different Voice: Taj os-Saltaneh." In *Women's Autobiographies in Contemporary Iran,* edited by Afsaneh Najmabadi, 17–31. Harvard Middle Eastern Monographs 25. Cambridge, Mass.: Harvard Univ. Press.

———. 1996. "Is Our Name Remembered?: Writing the History of Iranian Constitutionalism As If Women and Gender Mattered." *Iranian Studies* 29, nos. 1–2: 85–109.

———. 1998. "Crafting an Educated Housewife in Iran." In *Remaking Women: Feminism and Modernity in the Middle East,* edited by Lila Abu-Lughod, 91–125. Princeton: Princeton Univ. Press.

Olney, James. 1998. *Memory and Narrative: The Weave of Life-Writing*. Chicago: Univ. of Chicago Press.

Pascal, Roy. 1960. *Design and Truth in Autobiography*. Cambridge, Mass.: Harvard Univ. Press.

Perry, John R. 1996. "Persian in the Safavid Period: Sketch for an Etat de Langue." In *Safavid Persia,* edited by Charles Melville, 269–83. London: I. B. Tauris.

Pratt, Mary Louise. 1992. *Imperial Eyes: Travel Writing and Transculturation*. New York: Routledge.

———. 1995. "Comparative Literature and Global Citizenship." In *Comparative Literature in the Age of Multiculturalism,* edited by Charles Bernheimer, 58–65. Baltimore: Johns Hopkins Univ. Press.

Rezun, Miron. 1982. *The Iranian Crisis of 1941: The Actors: Britain, Germany and the Soviet Union.* Köln: Böhlau.

Rypka, Jan. 1968. *History of Iranian Literature.* Translated by Karl Jahn. Dordrecht, Holland: D. Reidel.

Sadiq, 'Isa. *Yadgar-i Omr.* Vol. 2. Tehran: Dihkhuda, 1976.

Savory, Roger. 1980. *Iran under the Savafids.* Cambridge: Cambridge Univ. Press.

———. 1995. "Tahlili az Tarikh va Tarikhnegari-yi Duran-i Safaviyih." *Iran Nameh* 13, no.3: 277–300.

Smith, Sidonie. 1998. "Performativity, Autobiographical Practice, Resistance." In *Women, Autobiography, Theory: A Reader,* edited by Sidonie Smith and Julia Watson, 108–15. Madison: Univ. of Wisconsin Press.

Sullivan, Zohreh. 1998. "Eluding the Feminist, Overthrowing the Modern?: Transformations in Twentieth-Century Iran." In *Remaking Women: Feminism and Modernity in the Middle East,* edited by Lila Abu-Lughod, 215–42. Princeton: Princeton Univ. Press.

Taj Al-Saltana. 1993. *Crowning Anguish: Memoirs of a Persian Princess from the Harem to Modernity 1884–1914.* Translated by Anna Vanzan and Amin Neshati. Washington, D.C.: Mage.

Taj al-Saltanah. 1991. *Khatirat-i Taj al-Saltanah.* Edited by Mansoureh Ettehadieh and Cyrus Sadounian. Bethesda, Maryland: Iran Books.

Taussig, Michael. 1993. *Mimesis and Alterity: A Particular History of the Senses.* New York: Routledge.

Tavakoli-Targhi, Mohamad. 1988. "The Formation of Two Revolutionary Discourses in Modern Iran." Ph.D. diss., Univ. of Chicago.

———. 1990. "Refashioning Iran: Language and Culture During the Constitutional Revolution." *Iranian Studies* 23, nos. 1–4: 77–101.

———. 1993. "Imagining Western Women: Occidentalism and Euro-Eroticism." *Radical America* 24, no.3: 73–87.

———. 1996. "Contested Memories: Narrative Structures and Allegorical Meanings of Iran's Pre-Islamic History." *Iranian Studies* 29, nos. 1–2: 149–75.

Wright, Denis. 1985. *The Persians Amongst the English: Episodes in Anglo-Persian History.* London: I. B. Tauris.

Yarshater, Ehsan. 1988. "The Indian or Safavid Style: Progress or Decline?" In *Persian Literature*, edited by Ehsan Yarshater. New York: Bibliotheca Persica, 1988.

———. 1989. "Communication." *Iranian Studies* 22, no.: 62–65.

Yeğenoğlu, Meyda. 1998. *Colonial Fantasies: Towards a Feminist Reading of Orientalism*. Cambridge: Cambridge Univ. Press.

Index